Super Cheap
Bora Bora
Travel Guide

"The beauty of Bora Bora isn't limited to its turquoise waters or green hills. That was mere surface beauty. " Sarah Jio, The Bungalow.

Our Mission

Did you know you can fly on a private jet for $500? Yes, a fully private jet. Complete with flutes of champagne and reclinable creamy leather seats. Your average billionaire spends $20,00 on the exact same flight. You can get it for $500 when you book private jet empty leg flights. Amazed? Don't be. This is just one of thousands of ways you can travel luxuriously on a budget.

When our brain hears the word "budget" it hears deprivation, suffering, agony, even depression. But budget travel need not be synonymous with hostels and pack lunches. You can enjoy an incredible and luxurious trip to Bora Bora on a budget, just like you can enjoy a private jet flight for 10% of the normal cost when you know how. The past years have shown us travel is a gift we must cherish. We believe strongly that this gift is best enjoyed on a budget. Together with thrifty locals, we have funneled our passion for travel bargains into Super Cheap Bora Bora.

Our passion is finding travel bargains. This doesn't mean doing less or sleeping in hostels. Someone who spends A LOT on travel hasn't planned or wants to spend their money. We promise you that with a bit of planning, you can experience a luxury trip to Bora Bora on a budget.

Traveling need not be expensive; Travel guides, Travel agents, Travel bloggers and influencers often show you overpriced accommodation, restaurants and big-ticket attractions because they earn commission from your "we're on vacation" mentality, which often leads to reckless spending. Our mission is to teach you how to enjoy more for less and get the best value from every dollar you spend in Bora Bora.

Taking a trip to Bora Bora is not just an outer journey, it's an inner one. Budget travel brings you closer to locals, culture and authenticity; which makes your inner journey more fulfilling.
Super Cheap Bora Bora will save you 1000 times what you paid for it while teaching you local tips and tricks. We have formulated

a system to pass on to you, so you can enjoy a luxurious trip to Bora Bora without the nightmare credit card bill.

Our mission is to dispel myths, save you tons of money, give you the local tips and tricks and help you find experiences in Bora Bora that will flash before your eyes when you come to take your last breath on this beautiful earth.

Who this book is for and why anyone can enjoy budget travel

There is a big difference between being cheap and frugal. Who doesn't like to spend money on beautiful experiences?

Over 20 years of travel has taught me I could have a 20 cent experience that will stir my soul more than a $100 one. Of course, sometimes the reverse is true, my point is, spending money on travel is the best investment you can make but it doesn't have to be at levels set by hotels and attractions with massive ad spends and influencers who are paid small fortunes to get you to buy into something you could have for a fraction of the cost.

This book is for those who want to have the cold hard budget busting facts to hand (which is why we've included so many one page charts, which you can use as a quick reference), but otherwise, the book provides plenty of tips to help you shape your own Bora Bora experience.

We have designed these travel guides to give you a unique planning tool to experience an unforgettable trip without spending the ascribed tourist budget.

This guide focuses on Bora Bora's unbelievable bargains. Of course, there is little value in traveling to Bora Bora and not experiencing everything it has to offer. Where possible, we've included cheap workarounds or listed the experience in the Loved but Costly section.

When it comes to FUN budget travel, it's all about what you know. You can have all the feels without most of the bills. A few days spent planning can save you thousands. Luckily, we've done the planning for you, so you can distill the information in minutes not days, leaving you to focus on what matters: immersing yourself in the sights, sounds and smells of Bora Bora, meeting awesome new people and feeling relaxed and happy. I sincerely hope our tips will bring you great joy at a fraction of the price you expected.

So, grab a cup of tea or coffee, put your feet up and relax; you're about to enter the world of enjoying Bora Bora on the cheap. Oh, and don't forget a biscuit. You need energy to plan a trip of a lifetime on a budget.

Super Cheap Bora Bora is <u>not</u> for travellers with the following needs:

1. You require a book with detailed offline travel maps. Super Cheap Insider Guides are best used with Google Maps - download before you travel to make the most of your time and money.
2. You would like thousands of accommodation, food and attraction recommendations; by definition, cheapest is often singular. We only include maximum value recommendations. We purposively leave out over-priced attractions when there is no workaround.
3. You would like detailed write-ups about hotels/Airbnbs/ Restaurants. We are bargain hunters first and foremost. We dedicate our time to finding the best deals, not writing flowery language about their interiors. Plus, things change. If I had a pound for every time I'd read a Lonely Planet description only to find the place totally different, I would be a rich man. Always look at online reviews for the latest up-to-date information.

If you want to save A LOT of money while comfortably enjoying an unforgettable trip to Bora Bora, minus the marketing, hype, scams and tourist traps read on.

Redefining Super Cheap

The value you get out of Super Cheap Bora Bora is not based on what you paid for it; it's based on what you do with it. You can only do great things with it if you believe saving money is worth your time. Charging things to your credit card and thinking 'oh I'll pay it off when I get home' is something you won't be tempted to do if you change your beliefs now. Think about what you associate with the word cheap, because you make your beliefs and your beliefs make you.

I grew up thinking you had to spend more than you could afford to have a good time traveling. Now I've visited 190 countries, I know nothing is further from the truth. Before you embark upon reading our specific tips for Bora Bora think about your associations with the word cheap.

Here are the dictionary definitions of cheap:

- Costing very little; relatively low in price; inexpensive: a cheap dress.
- costing little labor or trouble: Words are cheap.
- charging low prices: a very cheap store.
- Of little account; of small value; mean; shoddy: Cheap conduct; cheap workmanship.
- Embarrassed; sheepish: He felt cheap about his mistake.
- Stingy; miserly: He's too cheap to buy his own brother a cup of coffee.

Three out of six definitions have extremely negative connotations. The 'super cheap' we're talking about in this book is not shoddy, embarrassed, or stingy.
We added the super to reinforce our message. Super's dictionary definition stands for 'a super quality'. Super Cheap stands for enjoying the best on the lowest budget. Question other people's definitions of cheap so you're not blinded to possibilities, poten-

tial, and prosperity. Here are some new associations to consider forging:

Shoddy

Cheap stuff doesn't last is an adage marketing companies have drilled into consumers. However, by asking vendors the right questions cheap doesn't mean something won't last. I had a $10 backpack last for 8 years and a $100 suitcase bust on the first journey.

A study out of San Francisco University found that people who spent money on experiences rather than things were happier. Memories last forever, not things, even expensive things. And as we will show you during this guide, you don't need to pay to create glorious memories.[1]

Embarrassed

I have friends who routinely pay more to vendors because they think their money is putting food on this person's table. Paradoxically, Cuban doctors are driving taxis because they earn more money; it's not always a good thing for the place you're visiting to pay more and can cause unwanted distortion in their culture - Airbnb pushing out renters is an obvious example. Think carefully about whether the extra money is helping people or incentivising greed.

Stingy

Cheap can be eco-friendly. Buying thrift clothes is cheap, but you also help the Earth. Many travellers are often disillusioned by the reality of traveling since the places on our bucket-lists are overcrowded. Cheap can take you away from the crowds. You can find balance and harmony being cheap. "Remember a journey is

---

[1] Paulina Pchelin & Ryan T. Howell (2014) The hidden cost of value-seeking: People do not accurately forecast the economic benefits of experiential purchases, The Journal of Positive Psychology, 9:4, 322-334, DOI: 10.1080/17439760.2014.898316

best measured in friends, rather than miles." – Tim Cahill. And making friends is free!

A recent survey by Credit Karma found 50% of Millennials and Gen Z get into debt traveling. **Please don't allow credit card debt to be an unwanted souvenir you take home.** As you will see from this book, there's so much you can enjoy in Bora Bora for free, some many unique bargains and so many ways to save money! You just need to want to!

Discover Bora Bora

Bora Bora is the definition of a tropical getaway: Dreamy white sand beaches, blissful luxurious resorts, sunny skies, warm waters, and friendly locals.

The average nightly room rate for an overwater bungalow in Bora Bora is close to $1,000 USD, but don't despair this guide is going to show you the luxe life without having to cash in your retirement plan to pay for it, but first a bit of context. Bora Bora is a small South Pacific island northwest of Tahiti in French Polynesia. It is surrounded by sand-fringed motus (islets) and a turquoise lagoon protected by a coral reef. The island is just six miles long and 2.5 miles wide, every inch overflows with beauty.

The 18th-century British explorer James Cook coined Bora Bora the pearl of the Pacific. Since 1946, French Polynesia (a group of islands of which Bora Bora is a part) has been an overseas territory of France. But French Polynesia has a lot of autonomy, which you'll see in everything from their currency to taxation.

The official currency of Bora Bora is the French Pacific franc (CPF). One U.S. dollar (USD) is equivalent to about 115 CFP. In the 19th century Protestant missionaries came to the island, have heavily influenced religion in Bora Bora: Christianity continues to play a major role in the island's culture.

The main languages in Bora Bora are French and Tahitian, but you'll find that many people also speak English, especially resort staff. The major settlement, Vaitape, is on the western side of the main island, opposite the main channel into the lagoon. At the island's center rises Mt. Otemanu, a 727m dormant volcano.

Bora Bora's scuba diving is world-class, the area is home to three different kinds of sharks: the Blacktip, Whitetip and Grey reef shark. Its natural beauty and utter relaxation make it incomparable.

Bora Bora's main attraction is its lagoon. The color of the lagoon is a pastel blend of green and blue. The water is shallow and can be explored by a glass bottom boat or by diving. Bora Bora is home to the world's largest rays, Manta Rays. These rays are plankton eaters and regularly reside in the lagoon and they're safe to swim with.

The island is also home to a variety of tropical plants, including orchids. Many of the flowers have symbolic meanings. Coconuts are the island's main source of produce. Coconuts are also important in the Tahitian culture, with legends tied to the coconut trees.

The beaches, stunning free snorkelling, the mouth-watering seafood, don't be fooled by the glossy marketing brochures a luxurious trip to Bora Bora can be easily experienced on a budget. Your biggest Bora Bora cost is going to be getting to the island. There are limited flights to Bora Bora (only four per day), and they all originate in Tahiti. Hotels are few and fancy, ranging from $400–$2,000 per night for the lowest standard rates. The trick to keeping your trip affordable is to get off the tourist track, stay in cheaper overwater bungalows and take advantage of the local deals. If you follow the advice in this guide you could definitely get away with spending about $50 a day including accommodation making sure Bora Bora leaves a lasting impression on your heart and mind, not your bank balance.

Bora Borans move at a relaxed pace. Their life philosophy is 'Aita pea pea', which means not to worry, to go with the flow and enjoy life.

INSIDER CULTURAL INSIGHT

The locals call the island "Pora Pora" (meaning "first born"). The name Bora Bora comes from a misunderstanding. The 18th century European settlers misheard the islanders and Bora Bora has stuck.

Some of Bora Boras' Best Bargains

The cheapest overwater bungalows

Le Maitai Bora Bora offers the cheapest overwater bungalows in the whole of the French Polynesia. Prices start at $120 a night. If you're heart is set on staying in an overwater bungalow, this is the best price-performance you will find. It's $880 less a night than most overwater bungalows. The location is excellent. Beach access is literally across the street and the snorkelling experience will blow your mind. Visit to book direct for the lowest price.

There are only 13 over water bungalows at Maitai Polynesia. Each has a bedroom, a bathroom, and a terrace. They are decorated with Polynesian style decor. The bungalows are equipped with free wifi, comfortable beds, and a beautiful view of the lagoon. Book early.

Stay on a private Yacht

Consider booking a private Yacht inside of a hotel. Tahiti Yacht charters start from $70 per night per person. That's a $500 a night saving compared to an average overwater bungalow. You can just anchor in front of the nice hotels with over water huts and have the same scenery and swimming experience. You can also cook all your own food with supplies from the local markets. It works out very well if you have someone with sailing experience so you can also save on hiring a captain.

The island hopping pass

French Polynesia has over **118 islands** spread over 2,000 kilometers (1,200 mi) while most an uninhabited there are others worth seeing.

If you buy The island hopping pass from Air Tahiti you can save thousands. You'll get a 70% discount on what you'd pay if you book flights individually. Rather than just visiting Bora Bora, you can fly Tahiti to Maupiti, Raiatea, Huahine, Bora Bora, and back to Tahiti over the space of two weeks. The price is $400 for for seven flights to five islands, including Bora Bora. Meaning your flights into and out of Bora Bora cost just $60. The standard flight in is $200! https://www.airtahiti.com/en/airpass-fares

If you buy the island hopping pass check out the bonus section of free things to do in Maupiti, Raiatea and Huahine.

Cheaper resort packages

If your heart is set on a resort package in Bora Bora look at Costco Travel. They have resort packages from $2,000 per person. https://www.costcotravel.com/Vacation-Packages/Tahiti/Bora-Bora

Indulge in a fancy lunch for less

Le St James is 's hidden away in a tiny shopping centre in Vaitape. Don't let the location put you off. This French restaurant serves world-class food. The lunch menu is exceptional value for Bora Bora. A similar meal in a hotel will cost you $150 per person. With choices ranging from Lobster or steak with truffleflavoured purée for just $25! Reserve your table at: www.boraborastjames.com

Gorge on incredible sandwiches

L'Heure du Sud offer delicious and cheap well-stuffed sandwiches from a van parked in front of Le Petit Village shopping centre. Its the best bang for your buck eat you'll find on Bora Bora.

How to Enjoy ALLO-CATING Money in Bora Bora

'Money's greatest intrinsic value—and this can't be overstated—is its ability to give you control over your time.' - Morgan Housel

Notice I have titled the chapter how to enjoy allocating money in Bora Bora. I'll use saving and allocating interchangeably in the book, but since most people associate saving to feel like a turtleneck, that's too tight, I've chosen to use wealth language. Rich people don't save. They allocate. What's the difference? Saving can feel like something you don't want or wish to do and allocating has your personal will attached to it.

And on that note, it would be helpful if you considered removing the following words and phrase from your vocabulary for planning and enjoying your Bora Bora trip:

- Wish

- Want

- Maybe someday

These words are part of poverty language. Language is a dominant source of creation. Use it to your advantage. You don't have to wish, want or say maybe someday to Bora Bora. You can enjoy the same things millionaires enjoy in Bora Bora without the huge spend.

'People don't like to be sold-but they love to buy.' - Jeffrey Gitomer.

Every good salesperson who understands the quote above places obstacles in the way of their clients' buying. Companies create waiting lists, restaurants pay people to queue outside in order to create demand. People reason if something is so in demand, it must be worth having but that's often just marketing. Take this sales maxim 'People don't like to be sold-but they love to buy and flip it on its head to allocate your money in Bora Bora on things YOU desire. You love to spend and hate to be sold. That means when something comes your way, it's not 'I can't afford it,' it's 'I don't want it' or maybe 'I don't want it right now'.

Saving money doesn't mean never buying a latte, never taking a taxi, never taking vacations (of course, you bought this book). Only you get to decide on how you spend and on what. Not an advice columnist who thinks you can buy a house if you never eat avocado toast again.

I love what Kate Northrup says about affording something: "If you really wanted it you would figure out a way to get it. If it were that VALUABLE to you, you would make it happen."

I believe if you master the art of allocating money to bargains, it can feel even better than spending it! Bold claim, I know. But here's the truth: Money gives you freedom and options. The more you keep in your account and or invested the more freedom and options you'll have. The principal reason you should save and allocate money is TO BE FREE! Remember, a trip's main purpose is relaxation, rest and enjoyment, aka to feel free.

When you talk to most people about saving money on vacation. They grimace. How awful they proclaim not to go wild on your vacation. If you can't get into a ton of debt enjoying your once-in-a-lifetime vacation, when can you?

When you spend money 'theres's a sudden rush of dopamine which vanishes once the transaction is complete. What happens in the brain when you save money? It increases feelings of security and peace. You don't need to stress life's uncertainties. And having a greater sense of peace can actually help you save more money.' Stressed out people make impulsive financial choices, calm people don't.'

The secret to enjoying saving money on vacation is very simple: never save money from a position of lack. Don't think 'I wish I could afford that'. Choose not to be marketed to. Choose not to consume at a price others set. Don't save money from the flawed premise you don't have enough. Don't waste your time living in the box that society has created, which says saving money on vacation means sacrifice. It doesn't.

Traveling to Bora Bora can be an expensive endeavor if you don't approach it with a plan, but you have this book which is packed with tips. The biggest other asset is your perspective.

Planning your trip

When to visit

The first step in saving money on your Bora Bora trip is timing. The best times to go to Bora Bora are November and late April. These short shoulder seasons offer fine weather with temperatures in the mid-70s to mid-80s but most importantly the prices are lower than normal. High season runs from May to October, when rain showers are isolated. The wet season is from November to April with heavy humidity and a lot of cloud cover and mosquitoes (so bring repellent). But really anytime is a good time to visit Bora Bora, the weather is warm year-round.

Where to stay

I stayed at Villa Temanuata for $65 a night. We guests had access to a private beach in front of the bungalows, and it was a five-minute walk away from Matira Beach — the best beach on the main island. The added bonus: they offer a free pickup from the ferry terminal saving you $50 on a transfer.

If you decide to stay in the guesthouses, have cash ready. These guesthouses usually do not accept credit cards. So remember to withdraw enough money.

Before you book Check that your guesthouse has air-conditioning. The weather is hot and humid. And a room without A/C will make for uncomfortable nights.

The cheapest place to stay

Airbnbs/ guesthouses are the cheapest place to stay across the island. If you are craving the luxury resort experience (and who isn't?) supplement your Airbnb with five-star resort day passes.

That way you can experience all the luxury during the day and lay your head somewhere cheap at night. We will discuss the best day passes further on in the guide.

Chez Nono

Located on the white sands of Matira Beach, Chez Nono is an affordable guestshouse in Bora Bora. Accommodation options include two types of bungalows. One is located directly on the water and the other is in a wooden building with tropical decor. Guests have access to an outdoor swimming pool and a restaurant.

It is a short walk from a supermarket and a watersports center. This is one of the only watersports centers in the area. The guesthouse organizes excursions. It is also close to some major tour operators and Tahitian pirogues. Rooms start at $150.

Hack your Bora Bora Accommodation

Your two biggest expenses when travelling to Bora Bora are accommodation and food. This section is intended to help you cut these costs dramatically before and while you are in Bora Bora.

Hostels are the cheapest accommodation in Bora Bora but there are some creative workarounds to upgrade your stay on the cheap.

Use Time

There are two ways to use time. One is to book in advance. Three months will net you the best deal, especially if your visit coincides with an event. The other is to book on the day of your stay. This is a risky move, but if executed well, you can lay your head in a five-star hotel for a 2-star fee.

Before I travelled to Bora Bora, I checked for big events using a simple google search 'What's on in Bora Bora', there were no big events drawing travellers so I risked showing up with no accommodation booked (If there are big events on demand exceeds supply and you should avoid using this strategy) I started checking for discount rooms at 11 am using a private browser on booking.com.

Before I go into demand-based pricing, take a moment to think about your risk tolerance. By risk, I am not talking about personal safety. No amount of financial savings is worth risking that. What I am talking about is being inconvenienced. Do you deal well with last-minute changes? Can you roll with the punches or do you dislike it if something changes? Everyone is different and knowing yourself is the best way to plan a great trip. If you are someone that likes to have everything pre-planned using demand-based pricing to get cheap accommodation will not work for you. Skip this section and go to blind-booking.

Demand-based pricing

Be they an Airbnb host or hotel manager; no one wants empty rooms. Most will do anything to make some revenue because they still have the same costs to cover whether the room is occupied or not. That's why you will find many hotels drastically slashing room rates for same-day bookings.

How to book five-star hotels for a two-star price

You will not be able to find these discounts when the demand exceeds the supply. So if you're visiting during the peak season, or during an event which has drawn many travellers don't try this.

On the day of your stay, visit booking.com (which offers better discounts than Kayak and agoda.com). Hotel Tonight individually checks for any last-minute bookings, but they take a big chunk of the action, so the better deals come from booking.com. The best results come from booking between 2 pm and 4 pm when the risk of losing any revenue with no occupancy is most pronounced, so algorithms supporting hotels slash prices. This is when you can find rates that are not within the "lowest publicly visible" rate. To avoid losing customers to other websites, or cheapening the image of their hotel most will only offer the super cheap rates during a two hour window from 2 pm to 4 pm. Two guests will pay 10x difference in price but it's absolutely vital to the hotel that neither knows it.

Takeaway: To get the lowest price book on the day of stay between 2 pm and 4 pm and extend your search radius to include further afield hotels with good transport connections.

How to trick travel Algorithms to get the lowest hotel price

Do not believe anyone who says changing your IP address to get cheaper hotels or flights does NOT work. If you don't believe us, download a Tor Network and search for flights and hotels to one destination using your current IP and then the tor network (a tor browser hides your IP address from algorithms. It is commonly used by hackers). You will receive different prices.

The price you see is a decision made by an algorithm that adjusts prices using data points such as past bookings, remaining capacity, average demand and the probability of selling the room or flight later at a higher price. If knows you've searched for the area before ip the prices high. To circumvent this, you can either use a different IP address from a cafe or airport or data from an international sim. I use a sim from Three, which provides free data in many countries around the world. When you search from a new IP address, most of the time, and particularly near booking you will get a lower price. Sometimes if your sim comes from a 'rich' country, say the UK or USA, you will see higher rates as the algorithm has learnt people from these countries pay more. The solution is to book from a local wifi connection - but a different one from the one you originally searched from.

How to get last-minute discounts on owner rented properties

In addition to Airbnb, you can also find owner rented rooms and apartments on www.vrbo.com or HomeAway or a host of others. Nearly all owners renting accommodation will happily give renters a "last-minute" discount to avoid the space sitting empty, not earning a dime.

Go to Airbnb or another platform and put in today's date. Once you've found something you like start the negotiating by asking for a 25% reduction. A sample message to an Airbnb host might read:

Dear HOST NAME,

I love your apartment. It looks perfect for me. Unfortunately, I'm on a very tight budget. I hope you won't be offended, but I wanted to ask if you would be amenable to offering me a 25% discount for tonight, tomorrow and the following day? I see that you aren't booked. I can assure you, I will leave your place exactly the way I found it. I will put bed linen in the washer and ensure everything is clean for the next guest. I would be delighted to bring you a bottle of wine to thank you for any discount that you could offer.

If this sounds okay, please send me a custom offer, and I will book straight away.

YOUR NAME.

In my experience, a polite, genuine message like this, that proposes reciprocity will be successful 80% of the time. Don't ask for more than 25% off, this person still has to pay the bills and will probably say no as your stay will cost them more in bills than they make. Plus starting higher, can offend the owner and do you want to stay somewhere, where you have offended the host?

In Practice

To use either of these methods, you must travel light. Less stuff means greater mobility, everything is faster and you don't have to check-in or store luggage. If you have a lot of luggage, you're going to have fewer of these opportunities to save on accommodation. Plus travelling light benefits the planet - you're buying, consuming, and transporting less stuff.

Blind-booking

If your risk tolerance does not allow for last-minute booking, you can use blind-booking. Many hotels not wanting to cheapen their brand with known low-prices, choose to operate a blind booking policy. This is where you book without knowing the name of the hotel you're going to stay in until you've made the payment. This is also sometimes used as a marketing strategy where the hotel is seeking to recover from past issues. I've stayed in plenty of blind book hotels. As long as you choose 4 or 5 star hotels, you will find them to be clean, comfortable and safe. priceline.com, Hot Rate® Hotels and Top Secret Hotels (operated by lastminute.com) offer the best deals.

Hotels.com Loyalty Program

This is currently the best hotel loyalty program with hotels in Bora Bora. The basic premise is you collect 10 nights and get 1 free. hotels.com price match, so if booking.com has a cheaper price you can get hotel.com, to match. If you intend to travel more than ten nights in a year, its a great choice to get the 11th free.

Don't let time use you.

Rigidity will cost you money. You pay the price you're willing to pay, not the amount it requires a hotel to deliver. Therefore if you're in town for a big event, saving money on accommodation is nearly impossible so in such cases book three months ahead.

The best price performance location in Bora Bora

Restaurants and bars don't get that much cheaper the further you go from famous tourist attractions since the island is so small. Sunset Hill Lodge is a luxurious apartment hotel with consistent last-minute rooms from $30 a night.

How to be a green tourist in Bora Bora

As a volcanic island surrounded by an extensive coral reef complex Bora Bora is a fragile ecosystem. Thankfully Bora-Bora's government has implemented an effective plan to protect its reefs and reef resources. Its important as responsible tourists that we help not hinder Bora Bora in its battle to become sustainable.

There is a bizarre misconception that you have to spend money to travel in an eco-friendly way. This like, all marketing myths was concocted and hyped by companies seeking to make money off of you. In my experience, anything with eco in front of their names e.g Eco-tours will be triple the cost of the regular tour. Don't get me wrong sometimes its best to take these tours if you're visiting endangered areas, but normally such places have extensive legislation that everyone, including the eco and noneco tour companies, are complying with. The vast majority of ways you can travel eco-friendly are free and even save you money:

- Avoid Bottled Water - get a good water bottle and refill. The water in Bora Bora is safe to drink butask your hosts for confirmation as every accommodation may have a different water system.

- Thrift shop but check the labels and don't buy polyester clothes - overtime plastic is released into the ocean when we wash polyester.

- Don't put your shopping in a plastic bag, bring a cotton tote with you when you venture out.

- Pack Light - this is one of the best ways to save money. If you find a 5-star hotel for tonight for $10, and you're at an Airbnb or hostel, you can easily pack and upgrade hassle-free. A light pack equals freedom and it means less to wash.

- Travel around Bora Bora on Bikes or e-Scooters or use Public Transportation. Car Pool with services like bla bla car or Uber/Lyft share.

- Walk, this is the best way to get to know Bora Bora. You never know what's around the corner.

Saving money on Bora Bora Food

Create your own mini-bar

Beware, If you are staying in one of the over-water resorts, yo are a captive. It's hard to get to shops and supermarkets. Stock up on water, soda, juice, beer, wine, champagne, liquor and snacks at Tiare Market and Magasin Matira. They are the lowest priced supermarkets on Bora Bora and you can fill your mini bar for a one tenth of the price.

Breakfast

If you stay somewhere with a free breakfast, eat smart. Don't eat sugary cereals or white flour rich pastries if you don't want to be hungry an hour later. Before leaving your hotel or checking out, find some fresh fruit, water, and granola in the fitness centre or coffee in the lobby or business centre. If your hotel doesn't have free breakfast, don't take it. You can always eat cheaper outside. Aloe Cafe has the best cheap breakfast we found.

Wine
Non-French wine is overpriced in Tahiti. Plan on drinking French wine that is not aged.

Enjoy Tahitian Poisson Cru
It's raw tuna in coconut milk with line juices. It's truly unique to Tahiti and cheap!

SNAPSHOT: How to Enjoy a $10,000 trip to Bora Bora for $1,500

(full breakdown at the end of the guide)

Stay	Travelling in peak season: 1. Over-water bungalow at Le Maitai 2. Stay in a Beach front apartment for $65 3. Stay in a private room in a Airbnb if you want privacy and cooking facilities and low prices. Travelling in low season 1. Over-water bungalow at Le Maitai 2. Costco travel package 3. Last minute five-star hotel
Eat	Average meal cost: $10. Pizza and seafood are the best cheap eats here.
Move	Buy a Flight hopping pass for $500 Rent a bike to navigate Bora Bora for $10 a day
See	Beaches, diving, nature
Experience	Do a 4x4 Tour of the island, experience its fauna and flora and wildlife with expert guides for $80 Go Shark diving for just $95
Total	US$1,500

How to use this book

Google and TripAdvisor are your on-the-go guides while travel-ing, a travel guide adds the most value during the planning phase, and if you're without Wi-Fi. Always download the google map for your destination - having an offline map will make using this guide much more comfortable. For ease of use, we've set the book out the way you travel, booking your flights, arriving, how to get around, then on to the money-saving tips. The tips we or-dered according to when you need to know the tip to save mon-ey, so free tours and combination tickets feature first. We priori-tized the rest of the tips by how much money you can save and then by how likely it was that you could find the tip with a google search. Meaning those we think you could find alone are nearer the bottom. I hope you find this layout useful. If you have any ideas about making Super Cheap Insider Guides easier to use, please email me philgattang@gmail.com

A quick note on How We Source Super Cheap Tips
We focus entirely on finding the best bargains. We give each of our collaborators $2,000 to hunt down never-before-seen deals. The type you either only know if you're local or by on the ground research. We spend zero on marketing and a little on designing an excellent cover. We do this yearly, which means we just keep finding more amazing ways for you to have the same experience for less.

Now let's get started with juicing the most pleasure from your trip to Bora Bora with the least possible money!

OUR SUPER CHEAP TIPS...

Here are our specific tips for enjoying a $5,000 trip to Bora Bora for $1,200

How to Find Super Cheap Flights to Bora Bora

Luck is just an illusion. Anyone can find incredible flight deals. If you can be flexible you can save huge amounts of money. In fact, the biggest tip I can give you for finding incredible flight deals is simple: find a flexible job. Don't despair if you can't do that theres still a lot you can do. The following pages detail the exact method I use to consistently find cheap flights to Bora Bora.

Book your flight to Bora Bora on a Tuesday or Wednesday

Tuesdays and Wednesdays are the cheapest days of the week to fly. You can take a flight to Bora Bora on a Tuesday or Wednesday for less than half the price you'd pay on a Thursday Friday, Saturday, Sunday or Monday.

Start with Google Flights (but NEVER book through them)

I conduct upwards of 50 flight searches a day for readers. I use google flights first when looking for flights. I put specific departure but broad destination (e.g Europe) and usually find amazing deals.

The great thing about Google Flights is you can search by class. You can pick a specific destination and it will tell you which time is cheapest in which class. Or you can put in dates and you can see which area is cheapest to travel to.

But be aware Google flights does not show the cheapest prices among the flight search engines but it does offer several advantages

1. You can see the cheapest dates for the next 8 weeks. Other search engines will blackout over 70% of the prices.
2. You can put in multiple airports to fly from. Just use a common to separate in the from input.
3. If you're flexible on where you're going Google flights can show you the cheapest destinations.
4. You can set-up price tracking, where Google will email you when prices rise or decline.

Once you have established the cheapest dates to fly go over to skyscanner.net and put those dates in. You will find sky scanner offers the cheapest flights.

Get Alerts when Prices to Bora Bora are Lowest

Google also has a nice feature which allows you to set up an alert to email you when prices to your destination are at their lowest. So if you don't have fixed dates this feature can save you a fortune.

Baggage add-ons

It may be cheaper and more convenient to send your luggage separately with a service like sendmybag.com Often the luggage sending fee is cheaper than what the airlines charge to check baggage. Visit Lugless.com or luggagefree.com in addition to sendmybag.com for a quotation.

Loading times

Anyone who has attempted to find a cheap flight will know the pain of excruciating long loading times. If you encounter this issue use google flights to find the cheapest dates and then go to skyscanner.net for the lowest price.

Always try to book direct with the airline

Once you have found the cheapest flight go direct to the airlines booking page. This is advantageous in the current covid cancellation climate, because if you need to change your flights or arrange a refund, its much easier to do so, than via a third party booking agent.

That said, sometimes the third party bookers offer cheaper deals than the airline, so you need to make the decision based on how likely you think it is that disruption will impede you making those flights.

More flight tricks and tips

www.secretflying.com/usa-deals offers a range of deals from the USA and other countries. For example you can pick-up a round trip flight non-stop from from the east coast to johannesburg for $350 return on this site

Scott's cheap flights, you can select your home airport and get emails on deals but you pay for an annual subscription. A free workaround is to download Hopper and set search alerts for trips/ price drops.

Premium service of Scott's cheap flights.
They sometime have discounted business and first class but in my experience they are few and far between.

JGOOT.com has 5 times as many choices as Scott's cheap flights.

kiwi.com allows you to be able to do radius searches so you can find cheaper flights to general areas.

Finding Error Fares
Travel Pirates (www.travelpirates.com) is a gold-mine for finding error deals. Subscribe to their newsletter. I recently found a reader an airfare from Montreal-Brazil for a $200 round trip (mistake fare!). Of course these error fares are always certain dates, but if you can be flexible you can save a lot of money.

Things you can do that might reduce the fare to Bora Bora:--
• Use a VPN (if the booker knows you booked one-way, the return fare will go up)
• Buy your ticket in a different currency

The Cheapest route to Bora Bora from America

To get to Bora Bora you must first fly into French Polynesia's Faa'a International Airport. This is on Pape'ete, the capital of Tahiti. Air New Zealand, Air Tahiti Nui, Air France, LAN and Hawaiian Airlines all fly into Tahiti. From Papeete, Air Tahiti flies to 47 island air-strips.

French Bee is a budget airline with direct flights from San Francisco to Tahiti from $329. The flight takes 8 hours and 45 minutes.

Cheapest route from Europe

At the time of writing French Bee are flying to Bora Bora from Paris for $890 return.

If all else fails...

If you can't find a cheap flight for your dates I can find one for you. I do not charge for this nor do I send affiliate links. I'll send you a screenshot of the best options I found as airlines attach cookies to flight links. To use this free service please review this guide and send me a screenshot of your review - with your flight hacking request. I aim to reply to you within 12 hours. If it's an urgent request mark the email URGENT in the subject line and I will endeavour to reply ASAP. philgtang@gmail.com

Getting to the island

Arriving by air (via a 45-minute flight from the international airport in Pape'ete) is a breathtaking thrill as the island's towering jagged green peak, Mt. Otemanu jolts out surrounded on all sides by the clearest sparkling blue lagoon imaginable. That's the good news, the bad news is the cost. There is no way around it, a flight from Papeete to Bora Bora on the lone carrier that flies it ( ) can run between $200 (if you plan way in advance and buy a very restricted ticket) and $500+ round-trip. Unless you buy the island hopping pass and then it works out around $60.

The airport is on a beautiful motu (island), and accessible only by a short ferry ride to the port village of Vaitape. Resort transport is either by private motorboats from the airport operated by some of the luxury resorts or by shuttle from Vaitape.

INSIDER MONEY SAVING TIP
Air Tahiti offers 'kids fly free' if you fly from LAX as a family.

Cheaper than Bora Bora...

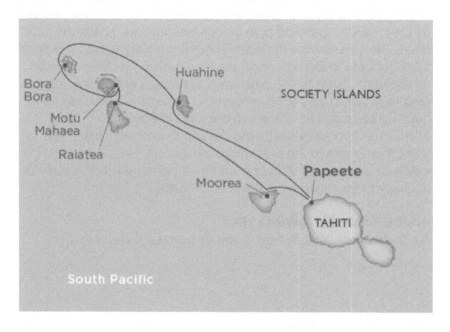

If you don't want to get the island hopping pass or pay the $500 round-trip from Pape'ete to Bora Bora I suggest you visit **Moorea**. While the island is growing in popularity, it still remains under the radar compared to Bora Bora but has the advantage of being easily and CHEAPLY reached. It's just a few kilometres of ocean from Tahiti, which has enabled a pair of ferry services to offer cheap crossings.

Insider Historical Insight

Tahitian legend about Bora Bora's formation

The legend goes one night a group of thieves tried to steal the island. They were pulling part of the island when they woke up a rooster, who scared the thieves enough that they dropped the part of the island they were pulling. They say that's why there's a 1.45 km² island called Toopua on the side of Bora Bora. It's the piece that was torn during the legendary burglary. Look at a map after listening and you'll see it.

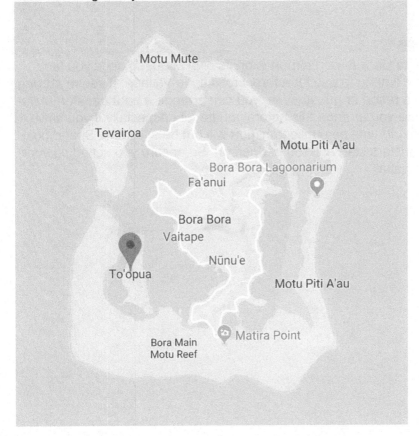

Arriving

Bora Bora Airport airport is on its own Motu, so once you land you'll need to pay for a ferry crossing to Vaitape. If you're staying in a resort or guesthouse, you can arrange a boat transfer. Make sure you arrange this before you travel - especially if you arrive at an odd time as public transport will not be available. Speed boat transfers start at $150 per person. So ensure you schedule your transfer.

Getting Around

The best way to get around Bora Bora is by bike. The entire island only takes a few hours to traverse. Rental cars are another option, but they cost significantly more than a rental bicycle. The local bus system, Le Truck, is notoriously unpredictable and taxis are extremely expensive.

I paid $10 a day for a blue bike with a basket to cycle around the island. While there is no regular scheduled public transportation system. Buses run in conjunction with schools or a ferry and cruises hours. The usual bus fare from Vaitape to Matira point is 500 CFX ($6). It's definitely worth asking at your guesthouse for more information, though, if you can't or don't want to cycle.

INSIDER MONEY SAVING TIP
Try Geocaching. This is where you hunt for hide-and-seek containers. You need a mobile device to follow the GPS clues in Bora Bora. A typical cache is a small, waterproof container with a logbook where you can leave a message or see various trinkets left by other cache hunters. Build

your own treasure hunt by discovering geocaches in Bora Bora.

Do your tours on Moorea

'Moorea is part of a chain of islands formed by hot spot volcanism; once an underwater volcano forms the island, it begins to erode and sink back into the ocean, meaning these islands are constantly changing.'

All tours on Moorea cost 50% less than what you would pay on Bora Bora. Mixing the two islands will give you the best bang for your buck especially if you want to go diving, snorkelling, jetski, do 4 wheel drives tours or other boat excursions.

Best things to do on Moorea

Visit the The Temae public beach

The Temae public beach is the longest beach on Moorea, and it is covered with coral corpses. It is accessible by a dirt road. The waters are translucent. Bring snorkel shoes because the coral corpses can be sharp.

Visit Tiahura Beach

he beach is a peaceful place to relax or picnic. The waters are protected by a reef, providing protection for stingrays and other marine life.

Visit Mareto Beach

Located on the northern coast of Moorea, Ta'ahiamanu Beach, also known as Mareto Beach, is one of the few beaches on the island that are open to the public. Despite its lack of sand, it's still a great place to swim and snorkel. The water is shallow and clear. The beach is also home to many hundreds of tropical fish. The shallow waters make it an ideal spot for kids to play. There's also a great selection of restaurants and shopping venues. It's also one of the best places to watch surfers carve up waves.

Visit Tipaniers Beach

Located at the tip of Opunohu Bay, Tipaniers Beach is a well-known beach in Moorea. It is perfect for swimming, snorkeling and watching sharks and rays.

Tipaniers Beach is a perfect place to rent a kayak. A kayak can be rented for $10 roundtrip. A kayak allows you to observe the beautiful coral gardens that surround the island.

Hike the Three Coconuts Pass Trail

This hiking trail will take you from the Belvedere Lookout, through the Opunohu Valley, and to a waterfall where you can take a refreshing dip. The Belvedere Lookout offers fantastic views of two of the bays on the island, as well as the peaks surrounding them. It's also a great place to hike.

Visit Ancient Polynesian temples
Thousands of years ago, the Polynesian people built stone temples known as marae. These were sacred temples where the people could perform religious ceremonies. These temples also served as a gathering place for the local community.

The Polynesian people believed that there were many gods. Each was responsible for different aspects of life. These gods could give mana, which was an essential force responsible for fertility and health. The gods were also responsible for giving mana to men, so the people could be successful in military campaigns.

The ancient Polynesian people worshiped at the temples and offered sacrifices to the gods. These temples are still visible today on the island of Moorea. The temples were surrounded by a low wall of crumbling rocks. They were also planted with trees. Trees were believed to have healing powers and would ward off evil spirits.

One of the oldest remains on the island of Moorea is the temple of Marae Titiroa. This is one of three remaining marae on the island. Marae Titiroa is a sacred site where canoes from all over the Pacific gathered in the mid-1990s for ceremonies celebrating the unity of the Polynesians.

Another important ancient Polynesian temple on Moorea is Marae Manunu. This temple was the center of social activity before the Europeans arrived in the 18th century. The Maohi ancestors of the Tahitians are believed to have lived here. The temple is now the main community marae for the Huahine people.

Another temple in Moorea is the restored Polynesian temple of Mara Arahurahu. This temple is located on the west coast of the island. It was the site of many island ceremonies in the past. It was also the site where Taiti, the last high priest of Maeva, was buried. All temples are free to visit.

Diving

Moorea is also known for its dive sites, which are located along the island's north side. Most dives are in caves or along slopes of the reef, and you can expect to see sea turtles and sharks. TOPDIVE Moorea offers the cheapest dive packages.

Dolphin Discovery Center

At $136 per person, this is definitely not super cheap however it is a great spot to see dolphins and turtles up close. The center offers free-diving with dolphins and turtle rehabilitation.

Why is the Coconut Important in Tahiti Culture?

Tahiti is home to many unique species of coconut trees, many of which are still protected by local laws. The coconut tree is one of the most common trees on the beaches of the islands. It provides food, drink, and fuel for the Polynesian people. Its pulp is rich in vitamins and nutrients. Coconuts are also used to make an indestructible rope, coconut sennit. Coconut oil played a major role in the Polynesian culture. The Polynesians carried it in their voyaging canoes and used it to protect themselves from the elements. The tree was also used for religious rites.

Explore Pape'ete

When you translate the Tahiti's capital city, Pape'ete to English you get 'basket of water'. This is a storied reference to how locals collected fresh water. In 1769, when James Cook anchored here, there was no settlement. Today 26,000 people call Pape'ete home. While the old colonial buildings are crumbling, one of the best things to experience on your way to or from Pape'ete is to visit street art in 'HANI'. It is a street full of colorful murals and graffiti art. Some of the most beautiful and iconic pieces can be found here including huge murals of beautiful Tahiti women with long flowing hair decorated in rare flowers. The murals are really a sight to behold and often cover up entire buildings and symbolise recent and historical events and topics. They are simply breathtaking - and of course free. Just google street art map of papeete tahiti and enjoy exploring.

Go to a free pearl museum

Visit is the Robert Wan museum. This Chinese-origin pearl producer developed pearls from shells in French Polynesia. He is known for his high-end jewelry. The museum has an impressive display of artifacts from the five archipelagos. And it's totally free.

Papeete Market

Papeete Market is one of the largest and most vibrant market places in French Polynesia. It offers a wide variety of local produce, including fresh fruits and vegetables. The market is filled with local vendors who sell handicrafts, clothing, and black pearls. There are also several Chinese bazaars.

The market is open from Monday through Saturday. It is located on Rue Francois Cardella, near the Tribal Pursuit and Police Municipale. The market is one of the oldest institutions in the archipelago.

The market is the best place to buy sarongs, pearls, and vanilla. It also offers traditional Polynesian food. It is a lively place that opens early in the morning and spills out into the nearby streets.

The market is divided into two floors. The lower level is filled with oils and Tahitian-made crafts. The upper level has a ripe fruit and vegetable market. The market also offers black pearl jewelry for a reasonable price.

Mahana Park beach

Mahana Beach is a popular destination for locals and tourists alike. Its calm and clear waters provide a perfect place for swimming and snorkeling. The beach is lined with palm trees, making it a great place to watch the sea life. There is also a handicraft shop and snack bar to enjoy.You can also find a playground and restrooms. During the summer months, locals and visitors alike can enjoy a picnic on the landscaped grounds.

There is also a surf break at Page de Taharuu, one of the safest on the island. The waves here regularly break at six to nine feet. This is a great place for beginner surfers to start.

For more action, visit the Arahoho Blowhole.

Hiking to Vaimahutu Falls

Fautaua Waterfall is one of the most impressive waterfalls in Tahiti. It is located in Fautaua Valley, and is more than 300 meters tall. The waterfall cascades into a pool with cool crystalline freshwater. The waterfall has been a sacred site in the island since ancient times.

The Te Pari trail starts at a French Army training center, which maintains the trail. Once you reach the top, you will have the opportunity to enjoy breathtaking views of the Pacific Ocean.

Hiking to this place will offer you the opportunity to see lush rainforest and three tall waterfalls. The hike is about three kilometers round trip. Bring mosquito repellent.

After the hike, you may want to spend some time in the natural swimming pool at the base of the waterfall. There are railings that protect the environment from the water.

Aside from the waterfalls, you can visit Papenoo Valley, a pristine valley. The valley is home to 160 small waterfalls. It is also close to archaeological sites and fruit trees.

Go to a black sand beach

'**Lafayette Beach**, a popular black sand beach near Papeete. Colored black because of the volcanic rock, Lafayette offers a different experience for those most familiar with classic white sand beaches.'

Visit botanical gardens

Tahiti has several botanical gardens. One of the most popular is the Mataoa Garden. This garden is home to tropical ferns that dangle from the cliff. The Harrison Smith Botanical Garden is stuuningly beautiful and totally free.

Visit La Plage de Maui

Among the best things to do on Tahiti is paying a visit to the dazzling white sands of La Plage de Maui. It is a sheltered lagoon with warm and clear water. It is located on the southern shore of the island, and is accessible by Tahitian roads. It is a popular beach on the island and is ideal for swimming. La Plage de Maui is also home to a lagoon-side snack bar, which serves fresh seafood. This beach is a little less secluded than the others in the area, but it's still a good place to spend the day.

Paofai Temple

Another popular place to visit in Papeete is the Paofai Temple. It is located near the Marina of Papeete. The temple is a blend of traditional architecture and local flavor and the largest Protestant church in Tahiti. You can attend a service lasting about 90 minutes with colorful singing, flower shirts and flower hats.

Marae Arahurahu Temple

Located on the west coast of Tahiti, the ancient Marae of Arahurahu is the best preserved Polynesian temple. In ancient times, the temple was a place of meetings and rituals. These were held for the purpose of worshiping the gods and influencing the harvest. The temple consisted of a low wall of basalt rocks, which was topped with an altar of vertical stones.

There were also stone pens near the entrance, which were used to keep pigs before sacrifices. The chief was also buried for nine months. The chiefs were considered sacred, so they could not be seen.

The old temple is now a place for reenactments of ancient Polynesian ceremonies during the Heiva Nui celebrations.

Eat Street Food in Pape'ete

Pork roasted in a firepit (ahima'a), fresh fish and seafood are the base for many tasty dishes accompanied by the staple starches Taro root, cassava or rice. Before you head to Bora Bora go to eat at **Place Vai'ete** in . You'll find a busy hub of street food vendors on the waterfront, known as roulottes. Each
one has its own cuisine and unique charm. Roulottes are frequented by locals and visitors alike. They're a casual and economical way to dine, and a perfect way to soak up the local culture. You'll find the freshest seafood including tuna salads caught that morning – dressed with coconut and cucumber.
Once your on Bora Bora, the food gets much more expensive and of a lessor quality so eat up at **Place Vai'ete!**

Taking a bus around Tahiti

Taking a bus around Tahiti can be a nice way to see more of the island. The main public transit system is a large white RTC motor coach. The buses are numbered and marked with the name of the village or district they serve. The route is usually a circular loop, but may be less convenient for longer trips.

Buses travel counterclockwise or clockwise around the island. The buses are painted green and white for the short distances and red and white for longer trips. They will stop at bus stops along the way.

Best Day Passes for the Five-star Experience

The two best day resort passes available on Bora Bora are Conrad Bora Bora Nui and The Intercontinental Hotel. They offer a day pass that allows you to use their private beach, pool, dressing rooms and includes a great lunch and a round-trip transfer from Vaitape from $80 a day depending on demand,

Conrad Bora Bora
Located on a private island off the main island of Bora Bora, the Conrad Bora Bora Nui Resort is a luxurious resort featuring an impressive lagoon. The Conrad Bora Bora Resort offers activities such as snorkeling tours and water sports. These are guided by marine biologists. Other complimentary activities include kayaking, paddleboards, and small catamarans. You can also learn the local Tahitian language for free there and enjoy other cultural activities.

The Conrad Bora Bora resort features four restaurants. The beachfront restaurant, Tamure Beach Grill, offers internationaland Polynesian food. The resort also has a modern Chinese restaurant. The menu includes seafood products from the Hainan Island, China's east coast.

The resort also has three bars. The first bar offers a poolside snack bar and the second bar has a swim-up bar. The third bar offers cocktails and other beverages.

Day passes start at $105.

Intercontinental Hotel
The Intercontinental Hotel (on Matira Beach) is a stunning resort that its worth buying a day pass for. 'L'InterContinental Bora Bora Le Moana Resort is located to the south side of the main island, at the famous Matira point, is considered one of the most beautiful beach in the world.' Day passes start at $80.

Most resorts in Bora Bora are amenable to offering day passes if they have capacity. Restrictions can be imposed if they have a large event such as a wedding. If you find a resort you like, simply call ahead to confirm availability. Prices range between $50 and $140 a day depending on demand.

Le Bora Bora (Ex Pearl Beach Resort) and Le Meridien Bora Bora are both worth investigating for day pass offers. They both offer exquisite 5-star luxury and great value day passes.

Discover Bora Bora's Wildlife

Bora Bora is a dormant volcano, it rose out of the middle of the ocean millenniums ago and all of its wildlife has migrated to the island over the past centuries. The few mammals that inhabit the island were brought over on ships by early inhabitants, including Bora Bora's healthy dog population. You will notice that most dogs on Bora Bora don't have owners but roam the streets and coexist peacefully with the people and tourists on the island. Bora Bora has a large number of exotic bird species, which the government of Polynesia protects to ensure their healthy future.

Look out for the Pacific Black Duck also known as Anas superciliosa. Of course, **The most incredible wildlife is the marine life.** Crabs roam the shores of the island while sea turtles, dol-

phins, and humpback whales tour the seas. There are 500 different species of fish swimming around the Tahitian islands.
The conditions are ideal for manta rays to flourish. Snorkelers
and scuba divers can easily spot the Gray Ray in waters near the
shore around the island. Pack your own travel snorkel equipment
and you'll have endless free entertainment.

Visit Pointe Tereia beach

Pointe Tereia beach is a quiet, secluded cove that offers views of the famous Motu Tevairoa. The water surrounding Pointe Tereia beach is shallow enough to allow snorkelers to see manta rays. If you pack a travel snorkel, you can have hours of fun here for free. And the beach is also bordered by mangroves, which are full of wildlife and there are two small restaurants.

Lounge on the best beach on the island

Matira Beach is a Serene, scenic beach featuring a stretch of white sand, plus clear aqua water with incredible snorkeling. The water is crystal clear, with temperatures in the high 70's/low 80's (depending on time of year).

'You'll find the beach about 5 miles south of Vaitape, and you can get there by bicycle or taxi. You can also drive there; you'll find parking spots near the InterContinental Bora Bora Le Moana Resort.'

Insider money saving tip
Snack Matira is within walking distance. Here you could grab a burger, french fries, and a couple of drinks for around $12. Half the price of most other nearby eateries and just as tasty.

See a Traditional Polynesian Dance

Tahiti has four different dance styles: ōte'a, aparima, hivinau and pa'o'a. The most popular one is ote'a. It is characterised by fast hip-shaking and soft arm movements.

Intercontinental Le Moana, Le Maitai Bora Bora and Sofitel Bora Bora Marara Beach all put on free shows. Check their websites for the schedule.

Aparima is more sensual and tells a story about falling in love. It uses intricate hand gestures and mimics everyday life. It was originally performed by men.

'Hivinau' is a Tahitian dance that is usually paired with pa'oa. The word hivinau means "to be happy," and the dancing is typically done in a double circle formation. The dance is accompanied by drums and chanting.

Visit Mount Otemanu

Mount Otemanu is the center piece of Bora's Bora's rich history It is one of two extinct volcanoes at the center of the island. Rising 2,400ft above the lagoon. It is awesome to see rain clouds at the peak of the mountain and clear blue skies surrounding it. You can enjoy Mount Otemanu by doing a 4x4 tour, a guided hiking trip, or just taking some casual snapshots on the beach.

For a 4x4 tour, **the Tupuna Safari 4x4 company takes travelers on a three-hour tour of Mount Otemanu and the rest of the island for $80 USD. Without doubt this is the best bang for your buck experience on Bora Bora if** you want to spend half a day seeing the very best of the island. You can book here: https://www.viator.com/tours/Bora-Bora/Bora-Bora-4WD-Tour/d5180-6769_4WD

Insider historical tip
'There are sacred areas on the mountain that contain the bodies of the ancient Polynesian Kings. If you look at Mount Otemanu from the southern side of the island you'll see massive circular stone walls of a temple which is said to house the king's spirit.'

Hike Mount Pahia

Mount Pahia is the second highest peak in Bora Bora. You can hike Mount Pahia in about an hour, and take in the stunning views of Mt Otemanu. The hike to the summit begins with a short ten-minute climb to the top of the mountain. From there, continue along the ridge to the lookout above Chez Guyette.

Don't miss sunsets

The sun setting in Bora Bora is a sight you shouldn't miss during your stay. Grab a drink a half hour before sunset, lay on a chaise lounge on the beach and just relax as the sky performs a dazzling dance in oranges, pinks and purples.

Pack a beach picnic

The cost of eating out can quickly add up if you're not doing day passes or you'll paying top dollar at tourist geared joints. For a meal that doesn't break the bank, prepare your own beach picnic. You can easily pack a watermelon to enjoy on the beach with a towel and a bottle of fizz. If you don't fancy preparing a picnic (hey, your on vacation!) go to Lucky House. This is a pizza place beside Temanuata with the best pizzas on the island. For $15, you'd get a large pizza which could easily feed two.

Go to Tiare Market

The Tiare Market is where locals go to shop. It's also the only store on the island with fishing gear. They have EVERYTHING. Snacks, food, appliances, toiletries, baby items. Here you can Stock up on fresh bread, croissants, and fruit for a third of the price. There was also a small store opposite Temanuata with cheap snacks if you just wanted to grab a bag of crisps or a chocolate bar.

Try a local beer called Hinano beer, its a 'bottom-fermented, golden-colored lager, with 5% alcohol content and pronounced bitterness.' It is both Cheap and delicious. A beer in a hotel will cost you $15.

Cheap local souvenirs

Municipal Market in Papeete sells fruit, vegetables, fish, oils, handicrafts, beautiful textiles and handcrafted items such as shell necklaces. It makes for a fun and eye-opening plunge into local culture and, unless you succumb to the persistent vendors, it will cost you nothing.

How much can you save haggling here?

Haggling is common at markets around the French Polynesians islands. Haggling in stores is generally unacceptable, although some good-humoured bargaining at smaller artisan or craft shops is not unusual if you are making multiple purchases.

Not super cheap but worth the fee

Bora Bora is expensive but these experiences are worth every cent…

Go swimming with sharks

You can swim with black tipped reef sharks and lemon sharks in waist-deep water, as well water that was 40m deep. The deep water was the cleanest, clearest, and most outstanding I've ever seen. This is the tour we booked -

The sharks in Bora Bora are not dangerous. They live under the green lagoons and are well acquainted with people. The lagoon is also a regular stop for manta rays, stingrays, and humpback whales during their migration to the warm waters of the South Pacific.

Visit the Lagoonarium

The Lagoonarium is an outdoor aquarium that specialises in displaying the fish and marine life of the Lagoon. It offers up close interaction with sharks and rays and even a chance to be pulled along by the fin of a shark. It costs $70US for a half day excursion, and go up to around **$100**US for a full day tour including lunch and time to relax at the beach.

Visit a Turtle Sanctuary

'The Islands of Tahiti aren't just a paradise for adventurous travelers, they also are home to some of our favorite sea creatures including whales, dolphins, sharks and sea turtles. From the end of September to the beginning of April, Green turtles come to lay eggs on the shore of the Tahitian beaches'

The Le Meridian has a unique care center for turtles – where you can observe these beautiful animals and learn firsthand about the rehabilitation process. It's 50 Euro per person. Green and Hawksbill turtles are the most common species you'll find there.

Explore the lagoon on a jet ski tour

This is a great way to get to know the island and its beautiful lagoon. You can even get close to sharks and stingrays! Prices start at $150.

Need to Know before you go

Currency: French Pacific franc
Language: French and Tahitian
Money: Available ATMs.
Visas: check http://www.doyouneedvisa.com **Time**: GMT -10
Important Numbers
113 Ambulance
112 Police

Watch to understand the History

Bora Bora 's history is fascinating. There are tons of documentaries. 15 Things You Didn't Know About Bora Bora is a great one to watch for free on YouTube before your visit. The short video contains a good set of relatively unknown facts about Bora Bora.

Cheap Eats

Eating in Bora Bora is known to be expensive. Dinner en-
trees cost between $30 and $70. Much of the seafood is
flown in from elsewhere as the casual locals tend to just fish
for themselves. The imported foods can be pricier than back
in your own country. Make the most of the fresh local Polynesian food and visit local markets discussed above. Combine that with these cheap eats where you can fill your
stomach without emptying your wallet by trying these local
restaurants on Bora Bora with mains under $15.

Note: Download the offline map on Google maps, (instruc-
tions 1. go to app 2. select offline apps in the left sidebar 3.
go to the area you want to download 4. click download).
Then simply type the restaurant names in to navigate, add it
to your favourites by clicking the star icon so you can see
where the cheap eats are when you're out and about to
avoid wasting your money at hyped tourist joints)

Roulotte Matira -Tahitian food truck with a permanent home in
Matira.
Snack Matira - on the Matira beach. Meals under $12.
Aloe Cafe
Is a Coffee Shop in the Centre commercial le pahia offering
Fresh food, delicious, at extremely cheap prices. They have
free wifi and great views.
Bloody Mary's Restaurant
Tasty seafood, nice and comfortable atmosphere, fast ser-
vice and cheap prices.
Bora Bora Yacht Club
Great views, and good seafood selection. Bora Bora Yacht
Club Restaurant is a laid-back, waterfront restaurant. The
menu offers dishes that combine Polynesian with French cui-
sine. You'll find fresh seafood, steaks, and carpaccio. This is
the perfect place to sit back and relax.

La Villa Mahana
Great music and even better food by chef Damien. Service is superb and prices are comparatively cheap.

La Matira Beach Restaurant
The food is delicious-full of flavor. And definitely a good place to go to for a cheaper meal, though not as cheap as Snack Matira.

Maikai Marina Yacht Club
The grilled fish here is one of the best things you'll eat on the island. Drinks are nice and prices were affordable.

Restaurant Fare Manuia
The pizzas are very good and taking into account that it's Bora Bora, the prices are not crazy expensive.

Fare Manuia
Wood fire pizzas for a low-price.

Bora Bora Pai Company
Food truck serving savoury turnovers.

Ben's
Ben's Cafe is the place to go for a variety of Tex Mex and American dishes. This restaurant is located right on Matira Beach, and is open from 8am to 5pm. Its menu includes burgers, spagetti, and hot dogs. You can even find a nice selection of fresh island fish.

Behrad Eats, a 24-hour taco stand.

Aloe Cafe, a cozy and convenient Internet cafe with cakes.

Craving something sweet?
Head to Iaorana Gelato for homemade Italian Ice Cream and great free WiFi.

Getting Out cheaply

At the time of writing Air Tahiti are offering the cheapest flights onwards.Take advantage of discounts and specials. Sign up for e-newsletters from local carriers including Air Tahiti to learn about special fares. Flights around the islands start at $150. **I strongly recommend you get the island hopping flight pass also form Air Tahiti.**

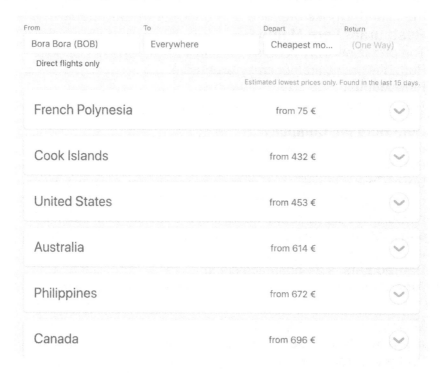

From	To	Depart	Return
Bora Bora (BOB)	Everywhere	Cheapest mo...	(One Way)
Direct flights only			

Estimated lowest prices only. Found in the last 15 days.

French Polynesia	from 75 €	⌄
Cook Islands	from 432 €	⌄
United States	from 453 €	⌄
Australia	from 614 €	⌄
Philippines	from 672 €	⌄
Canada	from 696 €	⌄

On your departure day, if you have a late flight you may be forced to check out well before leaving you without air conditioning.

Faa'a International Airport (PPT) is French Polynesia's only international airport. The airport is outdoors. The International Lounge is located one floor above the departure gates and entrance including air conditioning and free food and drinks will cost you $50 per person. For a relaxing time before you head home its actually worth it as the airport is humid and overcrowded.

Here are three methods you can use to access lounges at the airport:

- Get or use a credit card that gives free lounge access. NerdWallet has a good write-up about cards that offer free lounge access. www.nerdwallet.com/best/credit-cards/airport-lounge-access

- Buy onetime access. They start at $23 and often include free showers and free drinks and food.

- Find free access with the LoungeBuddy app. You pay an annual fee of $25 to use the app.

TOP TIP
If flying Air Tahiti, check in on line. There is a baggage drop line and a check in line. The baggage drop is 2 minutes, you could be in the check-in line for at least an hour.

Fully costed break-down

	How	Normal Cost without doing this	Cost when following suggested
How I got to Bora Bora	San Francisco for $600. I pre-purchased an island hop ping pass for $600	$3,500 upwards	$1,200
Get from the air port	Pre-arranged water taxi	speed boat trans-fers can run you $150 per person.	$25
Where I stayed	Airbnbs	Hotels are upwards of $650 a night.	$32 a night each sharing a room. Total cost for two weeks $448
Tastiest street foods I ate and cost	Fish in Papette. Pizza on bora bora.		$10 per meal
How I got around	biked $10 a day	$6 buses $50 taxi's per ride speed boat trans-fers can run you $150 per person.	$10 a day

What I saw and paid	snorkelling, jeep tour $80, island cruise $35m diving with sharks $95	The same tours on Bora Bora can be 3 times the price on Moorea. Pick your tours carefully to save thousands.	$200
Best dis counts	The local markets were the cheapest thing I came across		$10 for souvenirs
My Total costs	US$1,200		US$1,200

Print or screenshot for easy reference

	How	Cost
Get from the airport	Pre-arranged water taxi	$25
Stay	Airbnb or guest-houses for seven nights. I stayed in Moorea four nights and Bora bora for nine - my	$32 a night
Food	Average meal cost: $10 - see cheap eats section.	$10 per meal
Get around	Bike	$10 a day
See	Beaches, wildlife, sharks, diving, snorkelling.	$200
Best discounts	The local markets were the cheapest	
Get out	Use the island hopping pass and the return flight	$1,000
Total	US$1,500	US$1,500

PRACTICAL THINGS TO REMEMBER TO SAVE MONEY ON YOUR BORA BORA VACATION.

Transfer Pacific Francs (XCF) to a prepaid debit card. This will save you a lot on transaction fees and exchange rates.

Bring liquor if you plan to drink. You should be able to take 2 750 ml bottles of liquor and 2 750 ml bottles of wine per person. Immigration / customs in Tahiti is somewhere between lax and non-existent.

Bring a cold bag. Ice is readily available on the resorts, but refrigeration is not. A collapsible Yeti-style cooler will be great for enjoying cold beers on the beach.

Download google maps for use offline. This is very useful for cycling around the island. If you plan to hike provides the best offline detailed maps.

The mosquitos are quite bad on Bora Bora so bring a good mosquito spray or combine a few drops of lemongrass oil with a moisturiser (but make sure you rub everywhere)/ This is the technique the Inca's used to keep mosquitos at bay. The smell turns the mosquitos around.

The sun is very harsh, a good REEF FRIENDLY sun cream is essential

Download the French language pack on google translate - you will be grateful you have it! Not many people speak English outside of the tourist hotspots but all speak French.

It's very humid so if you're not used to the heat, ensure your accommodation has AC.

Plan to spend a day in Papeete just for the incredible (and cheap) street food.

Analyse if the island hopping pass is worth it for your trip.

Book your airbnbs or overwater bungalows.

Book any tours you might want to do on Moorea, you can take the ferry there cheaply from Papeete

Decide which resorts you might want to go to visit with day passes on Bora Bora.

Pre-arrange your transfer with your accommodation providers from Bora Bora airport if you are arriving at an odd time.

Pack a travel snorkel kit if you plan to snorkel. Its a great free activity when you have your own equip ment and gives you greater flexibility to hire a boat and go snorkelling alone.

What to Pack:

- swimsuits/ trunks
- 'throw over' sun shirt/s to prevent sunburn.
- light weight clothing - sun dresses, t-shirts, shorts.
- lightweight waterproof/windproof jacket.
- sun hat that can scrunch up in your bag, get wet, and won't blow off in the wind.

RECAP: How to Enjoy a $10,000 trip to Bora Bora for $1,500

Find a cheap flight
Using the strategy we outlined you can snag a ticket to Bora Bora from the states from $600 return with French bee. From Europe its a longer trip, so more expensive but you'll find deals from Paris. Potential saving $2,000.

Buy an island hopping pass
It works out basically the same price as a return to Bora Bora. Potential saving $2,000

Sleep cheap and visit 5-star resorts on day passes
Instead of paying $1,000 + a night, stay in a cheap over water bungalow, airbnb or guesthouse and save $800 A NIGHT! Potential saving $5,600

Eat at the markets
If you're on a budget, but like eating out, consider doing your dining on the streets. The food is equally as Delicious as a sit-down restaurant, just go where there are crowds. Potential saving $100.

Do your tours on Moorea
50% cheaper than Bora Bora. Plain and simple. Potential savings: $600.

Do all the free stuff first
The natural environment in Bora Bora is an endless bounty of interesting and inspiring things to experience. Start free and be mindful of what you want to pay for. Like any tourist place you can easily part with money you didn't need to. Potential savings: $1,200.

Check your credit card for free access to the Tahiti airport lounge
The airport is outside and its worth paying the $50 for aircon and relaxation.

Money Mistakes in Bora Bora

Cost	Impact	Solution	Note
Using your home currency	Some credit card rates charge for every transaction in another currency. Check carefully before you use it	Use a prepaid currency card like Wise Multi-Currency Debit Card.	If you wouldn't borrow money from a friend or relative for your trip, don't borrow it from a credit card company.
Not booking tours ahead of time	If you visit during peak times tours will be booked up and those available will be expensive.	Prebook your tours. Costo Travel have cheap packages and Moorea offers the same tours for half the price.	
Renting sunloungers	$20 for two rentals. This cost can take a silent bite out of your budget.	Bring a compact beach sofa. Many fit into hand luggage.	
Buying bottled water	At $3 a bottle, this is a cost that can mount up quickly	Bring an on the go water filter bottle like Water-to-go.	
Eating like a tourist	Eating at tourist traps can cost you dearly in Bora Bora. Choose wisely	Star cheap eats on google maps so you're never far from one	
Forgetting essenitals	Becaus Bora Bora is an island foregtting sunscreen, after sun and other essentials can cost you $30 per bottle	Pack your essentials to last the duration of your trip.	
Not agreeing a price of everything in advance	Taxi's and other unpriced services allow people to con you..	Agree the price beforehand to avoid unwanted bills	

Bonus: Free things to do on Raiatea, Maupiti and Huahine

If you pay the island hopping pass, here are some ways to save money on Raiatea, Maupiti and Huahine.

Free Things to Do in Raiatea

Tiare Apetahi

The big picture: Raiatea is the second largest island in the archipelago, and it is a little less touristy than Bora Bora. It also has the tallest peak of the archipelago, Mount Temehani. Its other names include the "Sacred Island," and the "Mounting Place of the Sun." It is the cradle of Polynesian culture, and it is home to some of the world's best snorkeling, diving, and surfing.

Visit the Taputapuatea Marae

Visiting the Taputapuatea Marae in Raiatea Island is one of the free things to do in Raiatea. This ancient temple is an important cultural and spiritual site for Polynesian culture. This is considered the oldest archaeological site in Polynesia. It is also classified as a UNESCO World Heritage Site.

Taputapuatea Marae was once a ceremonial and political site. It is thought that it dates back to about 1000 AD. The site is believed to have been used as a meeting point for the priests and navigators. It was later used as a place of burial.

Go hiking

The island of Raiatea is home to several endemic species of plants and animals. This is an area of great interest for scientists. The island also hosts many waterfalls.

There are several trails to choose from: Raiatea - Mount Temehani and the Taputapuatea marae.Another great hike in Raiatea is a hike from Uturoa to Mount Tapioi. This hike includes swimming opportunities and a chance to see three waterfalls. A round trip takes approximately eight hours.

Explore the sacred Mt Temehani Plateau

The biggest attraction on this tropical island is the Temehani Plateau, the only place in the world where the rarest flower, the Tiare Apetahi, grows. It is a flower with five petals. It grows only on Raiatea, and it is forbidden to pick it.

Botanical Garden of Faaroa

The botanical garden is a great place to learn about the island's floral wealth and its totally free. Visitors can take a free guided tour and learn about the various plants. There are also some informative panels that explain the island's floral wealth.

River Cruise

The Faaroa River is a French Polynesian river that is navigable. You can explore it on a guided kayak excursion. Located at the Raiatea Lodge Hotel ($200 a night), this excursion is free to guests. You'll get a glimpse of Raiatea's lush jungle interior, as well as its rich history.

Free Things to Do in Maupiti

The island is known for having defeated hotel groups to keep its authenticity. There are plenty of things to do and see, from swimming to snorkeling to scuba diving. It is also home to the largest volcano in French Polynesia and is known for its teeming number of petroglyphs.

Manta ray 'cleaning station'

Visiting the Manta ray 'cleaning station' near the Onoiau pass, south of Maupiti is one of the most fascinating things to do in Maupiti. These majestic creatures come to this station for skin cleaning.

Their bodies are littered with parasites and dead skin, and cleaner fish help them by eating it.

This is a naturally occurring phenomenon, and is helpful to both the rays and the cleaner fish.

Manta rays spend hours at a time in the water at a cleaning station, and they return to the same place year after year. In order to keep their health and appearance in top condition.

Manta rays and cleaner fish live in a symbiotic relationship, and a cleaning station is a good example of this.

Manta ray cleaning stations are a major draw in Palau. They are also an important study location for manta rays.

You can snorkel at a manta ray 'cleaning station'. However, it is best to heed the code of conduct and not touch any mantas while you are watching.

Hiking

Hiking is one of the best things to do in Maupiti. You'll want to check out Mount Teurafaatiu, the island's highest peak. It offers spectacular views of the lagoon and surrounding motus.

It takes about an hour to get to the top. Once you get to the top, you'll find views of Bora Bora and the surrounding motus.

One of the most popular hikes in Maupiti is the Three Coconuts hike. It's easy to do with a light pack. You can hike from one end of the island to the other, then connect to the Ha'apiti hike on the south coast. You can also combine the Three Coconuts hike with the Afareaitu Falls hike for even more adventure.

You can also see the local market. It's located near the municipal buildings. It's a great place to pick up some fresh fruit and baked snacks for hikes.

Free Things to Do in Huahine

Huahine is a small island also known as the "woman island." It is a lush green island with a beautiful lagoon. It is home to many ancient Polynesian ruins. If you're a nature lover, you'll love the beaches, hiking, and snorkeling. If you're looking for adventure, you'll be able to enjoy a hike to a waterfall or go fishing.

Huahine is a great place for backpackers. You can stay in a three-star hotel or a budget pension from $50 and it has some of the best restaurants in the Pacific.

The locals support themselves through small-scale farming and fishing. They operate pensions and produce stands. The main strip along the water-front is lined with small boutiques and a bustling supermarket.

Beaches

You can explore the Fare public beach on Huahine Nui. This beach offers a stunning silhouette of a re-clining woman. The beach is also home to ancient Polynesian structures. These structures provide visitors with a glimpse into the pre-European civi-lization.

The Huahine Museum

The Huahine Museum is a great place to learn about the island's history. Entrance fee 250f $2.

See Sacred blue-eyed eels for free

Sacred blue-eyed eels are a famous attraction in Huahine. You can visit them in the village of Faie. These long-finned Polynesian eels are about four to six feet long and come in bright blue.

These eels are also known for their huge gills. They eat trash and bacteria on the river bed. They are also sacred to the islanders. They are believed to carry the spirits of the dead islanders.

A short walk from the village of Faie is a river where blue-eyed eels live. The locals have been feeding them for years. Visitors can view them from the bridge. They can also hand feed them.

Ancient Polynesian ruins

You can visit dozens of ancient Polynesian ruins. These ruins once served as religious temples. They were also sites of sacrifice. The temples were built in honor of polynesian gods. Many of these temples have been restored. You can see many of the ruins for free.

One of the most important archaeological sites on Huahine is the Maeva Settlement. It is home to the largest concentration of ancient Polynesian ruins in the Pacific. It has been restored and is listed by UNESCO.

The Maeva Settlement was the center of religious life for the ancient Polynesian people. The ancient Tahitians worshipped at stone temples called marae. These temples are located around the village of Maeva. You can explore them on walking trails. There are 30 temples in the Maeva marae complex. You can combine the visit to the museum with the marae tour.

Explore art shops

Huahine offers a number of art shops around the island. One of these is Gallery Umatatea. This gallery is located on Motu Ovarei, past the village of Maeva.

The secret to saving HUGE amounts of money when travelling to Bora Bora is...

Your mindset. Money is an emotional topic, if you associate words like cheapskate, Miser (and its £9.50 to go into Charles Dickens Bora Bora house, oh the Irony) with being thrifty when traveling you are likely to say 'F-it' and spend your money needlessly because you associate pain with saving money. You pay now for an immediate reward. Our brains are prehistoric; they focus on surviving day to day. Travel companies and hotels know this and put trillions into making you believe you will be happier when you spend on their products or services. Our poor brains are up against outdated programming and an onslaught of advertisements bombarding us with the message: spending money on travel equals PLEASURE. To correct this carefully lodged propaganda in your frontal cortex, you need to imagine your future self.

Saving money does not make you a cheapskate. It makes you smart. How do people get rich? They invest their money. They don't go out and earn it; they let their money earn more money. So every time you want to spend money, imagine this: while you travel, your money is working for you, not you for money. While you sleep, the money, you've invested is going up and up. That's a pleasure a pricey entrance fee can't give you. Thinking about putting your money to work for you tricks your brain into believing you are not withholding pleasure from yourself, you are saving your money to invest so you can go to even more amazing places. You are thus turning thrifty travel into a pleasure fueled sport.

When you've got money invested - If you want to splash your cash on a first-class airplane seat - you can. I can't tell you how to invest your money, only that you should. Saving $20 on taxis doesn't seem like much, but over time you could save upwards of $15,000 a year, which is a deposit for a house which you can rent on Airbnb to finance more travel. Your brain making money looks like your brain on cocaine, so tell yourself saving money is making money.

Scientists have proved that imagining your future self is the easiest way to associate pleasure with saving money. You can download FaceApp — which will give you a picture of what you will look like older and grayer, or you can take a deep breath just before spending money and ask yourself if you will regret the purchase later.

The easiest ways to waste money traveling are:

Getting a taxi. The solution to this is to always download the google map before you go. Many taxi drivers will drive you around for 15 minutes when the place you were trying to get to is a 5-minute walk… remember while not getting an overpriced taxi to tell yourself, 'I am saving money to free myself for more travel.' Spending money on overpriced food when hungry. The solution: carry snacks. A banana and an apple will cost you, in most places, less than a dollar.

Spending on entrance fees to top-rated attractions. If you really want to do it, spend the money happily. If you're conflicted, sleep on it. I don't regret spending $200 on a sky dive over the Great Barrier Reef; I regret going to the top of the shard on a cloudy day in London for $60. Only you can know, but make sure it's your decision and not the marketing directors at said top-rated attraction.

Telling yourself 'you only have the chance to see/eat/experience it now'. While this might be true, make sure YOU WANT to spend the money. Money spent is money you can't invest, and often you can have the same experience for much less.

You can experience luxurious travel on a small budget, which will trick your brain into thinking you're already a high-roller, which will mean you'll be more likely to act like one and invest your money. Stay in five-star hotels for $5 by booking on the day of your stay on booking.com to enjoy last-minute deals. You can go to fancy restaurants using daily deal sites. Ask your airline about last-minute upgrades to first-class or business. I paid $100 extra on a $179 ticket to Cuba from Germany to be bumped to Business Class. When you ask, it will surprise you what you can get both at hotels and airlines.

Travel, as the saying goes, is the only thing you spend money on that makes you richer. You can easily waste money, making it difficult to enjoy that metaphysical wealth. The biggest money saving secret is to turn bargain hunting into a pleasurable activity, not an annoyance. Budgeting consciously can be fun, don't feel disappointed because you don't spend the $60 to go into an attraction. Feel good because soon that $60 will soon earn money for you. Meaning, you'll have the time and money to enjoy more metaphysical wealth while your bank balance increases.

So there it is. You can save a small fortune by being strategic with your trip planning. We've arranged everything in the guide to offer the best bang for your buck. Which means we took the view that if it's not an excellent investment for your money, we wouldn't include it. Why would a guide called 'Super Cheap' include lots of overpriced attractions? That said, if you think we've missed something or have unanswered questions, ping me an email: philgtang@gmail.com I'm on central Europe time and usually reply within 8 hours of getting your mail. We like to think of our guide books as evolving organisms helping our readers travel better cheaper. We use reader questions via email to update this book year round so you'll be helping other readers and yourself.

Don't put your dreams off!

Time is a currency you never get back and travel is its greatest return on investment. Plus, now you know you can visit Bora Bora for a fraction of the price most would have you believe.

Thank you for reading

Dear **Lovely Reader**,

If you have found this book useful, please consider writing a quick review on Amazon.

One person from every 1000 readers leaves a review on Amazon. It would mean more than you could ever know if you were one of our 1 in 1000 people to take the time to write a brief review.

Thank you so much for reading again and for spending your time and investing your trips future in Super Cheap Insider Guides. One last note, please don't listen to anyone who says 'Oh no, you can't visit Bora Bora on a budget'. Unlike you, they didn't have this book. You can do ANYWHERE on a budget with the right insider advice and planning. Sure, learning to travel to Bora Bora on a budget that doesn't compromise on anything or drastically compromise on safety or comfort levels is a skill, but this guide has done the detective work for you. Now it is time for you to put the advice into action.

Phil and the Super Cheap Insider Guides Team

P.S If you need any more super cheap tips we'd love to hear from you e-mail me at philgtang@gmail.com, we have a lot of contacts in every region, so if there's a specific bargain you're hunting we can help you find it.

DISCOVER YOUR NEXT VACATION

☑ LUXURY ON A BUDGET APPROACH

☑ CHOOSE FROM 107 DESTINATIONS

☑ EACH BOOK PACKED WITH REAL-TIME LOCAL TIPS

All are available in Paperback and e-book on Amazon: https://www.amazon.com/dp/B09C2DHQG5

Several are available as audiobooks. You can watch excerpts of ALL for FREE on YouTube: https://youtube.com/channel/UCx-o9YV8-M9P1cFosU-Gjnqg

Super Cheap ADELAIDE 2023
Super Cheap ALASKA 2023
Super Cheap AMSTERDAM 2023
Super Cheap ANTIGUA 2023
Super Cheap ANTARCTICA 2023
Super Cheap AUSTIN 2023
Super Cheap BANGKOK 2023
Super Cheap BARBADOS 2023
Super Cheap BARCELONA 2023
Super Cheap BATH 2023
Super Cheap BELFAST 2023
Super Cheap BERMUDA 2023
Super Cheap BERLIN 2023
Super Cheap BORDEAUX 2023
Super Cheap BRUGES 2023
Super Cheap BUDAPEST 2023
Super Cheap Bahamas 2023
Super Cheap Great Barrier Reef 2023
Super Cheap CABO 2023

Super Cheap CALGARY 2023
Super Cheap CAMBRIDGE 2023
Super Cheap CANCUN 2023
Super Cheap CAPPADOCIA 2023
Super Cheap CAPRI 2023
Super Cheap CARCASSONNE 2023
Super Cheap CHAMPAGNE REGION 2023
Super Cheap CHIANG MAI 2023
Super Cheap CHICAGO 2023
Super Cheap COPENHAGEN 2023
Super Cheap DOHA 2023
Super Cheap DOMINICAN REPUBLIC 2023
Super Cheap DUBAI 2023
Super Cheap DUBLIN 2023
Super Cheap EDINBURGH 2023
Super Cheap FLORENCE 2023
Super Cheap GALAPAGOS ISLANDS 2023
Super Cheap GALWAY 2023
Super Cheap HAVANA 2023
Super Cheap HELSINKI 2023
Super Cheap HONG KONG 2023
Super Cheap HONOLULU 2023
Super Cheap INNSBRUCK 2023
Super Cheap ISTANBUL 2023
Super Cheap KUALA LUMPUR 2023
Super Cheap LA 2023
Super Cheap LAPLAND 2023
Super Cheap LAS VEGAS 2023
Super Cheap LIMA 2023
Super Cheap LISBON 2023
Super Cheap LIVERPOOL 2023
Super Cheap LONDON 2023
Super Cheap MACHU PICHU 2023
Super Cheap MALAGA 2023
Super Cheap MALDIVES 2023

Super Cheap Machu Pichu 2023
Super Cheap MELBOURNE 2023
Super Cheap MIAMI 2023
Super Cheap MONACO 2023
Super Cheap Milan 2023
Super Cheap Munich 2023
Super Cheap NASHVILLE 2023
Super Cheap NEW ORLEANS 2023
Super Cheap NEW YORK 2023
Super Cheap NORWAY 2023
Super Cheap PARIS 2023
Super Cheap PRAGUE 2023
Super Cheap SAN FRANCISCO 2023
Super Cheap Santorini 2023
Super Cheap SEYCHELLES 2023
Super Cheap SINGAPORE 2023
Super Cheap SYDNEY 2023
Super Cheap ST LUCIA 2023
Super Cheap TORONTO 2023
Super Cheap TURKS AND CAICOS 2023
Super Cheap TURIN 2023
Super Cheap VENICE 2023
Super Cheap VIENNA 2023
Super Cheap WASHINGTON 2023
Super Cheap YORK 2023
Super Cheap YOSEMITE 2023
Super Cheap ZURICH 2023
Super Cheap ZANZIBAR 2023

Bonus Travel Hacks

I've included these bonus travel hacks to help you plan and enjoy your trip to Bora Bora cheaply, joyfully, and smoothly. Perhaps they will even inspire you to start or renew a passion for long-term travel.

Common pitfalls when it comes to allocating money to <u>your desires</u> while traveling

Know the exchange rate

If you're traveling from the states to Indonesia, your one dollar is worth 10,1,200 rupiah. When your is wallet stuffed with high-denomination bills, you'll less likely to remember the exchange rate. Remember, it's not monopoly money, it's your money and you should consciously choose to spend it on things you desire. At the time of writing, 1 dollar is Bora Bora in 115 CFP.

Beware of Malleable mental accounting

Let's say you budgeted spending only $30 per day in Bora Bora but then you say well if I was at home I'd be spending $30 on food as an everyday purchase so you add another $30 to your budget. Don't fall into that trap as the likelihood is you still have expenses at home even if its just the cost of keeping your freezer going.

Beware of impulse purchases in Bora Bora

Restaurants that you haven't researched and just idle into can sometimes turn out to be great, but more often, they turn out to suck, especially if they are near tourist attractions. Make yourself a travel itinerary including where you'll eat breakfast and lunch. Dinner is always more expensive, so the meal best to enjoy at home or as a takeaway. This book is full of incredible cheap eats. All you have to do is plan to go to them.

Social media and FOMO (Fear of Missing Out)

'The pull of seeing acquaintances spend money on travel can often be a more powerful motivator to spend more while traveling than seeing an advertisement.' Beware of what you allow to influence you and go back to the question, what's the best money I can spend today?

Now-or-never sales strategies

One reason tourists are targeted by salespeople is the success of the now-or-never strategy. If you don't spend the money now… your never get the opportunity again. Rarely is this true.

Instead of spending your money on something you might not actually desire, take five minutes. Ask yourself, do I really want this? And return to the answer in five minutes. Your body will either say an absolute yes with a warm, excited feeling or a no with a weak, obscure feeling.

Unexpected costs

"Holding on to anger is like grasping a hot coal with the intent of throwing it at someone else; you only hurt yourself." The Buddha.

One downside to traveling is unexpected costs. When these spring up from airlines, accommodation providers, tours and on and on, they feel like a punch in the gut. During the pandemic my earnings fell to 20% of what they are normally. No one was traveling, no one was buying travel guides. My accountant out of nowhere significantly raised his fee for the year despite the fact there was a lot less money to count. I was so angry I consulted a lawyer who told me you will spend more taking him to court than you will paying his bill. I had to get myself into a good feeling place before I paid his bill, so I googled how to feel good paying someone who has scammed you.

The answer: Write down that you will receive 10 times the amount you are paying from an unexpected source. I did that. Four months later, the accountant wrote to me. He had applied for a COVID subsidy for me and I would receive... you guessed it almost exactly 10 times his fee.

Make of that what you want. I don't wish to get embroiled in a conversation about what many term 'woo-woo', but the result of my writing that I would receive 10 times the amount made me feel much, much better when paying him. And ultimately, that was a gift in itself. So next time some airline or train operator or hotel/ Airbnb sticks you with an unexpected fee, immediately write that you will receive 10 times the amount you are paying from an unexpected source. Rise your vibe and skip the added price of feeling angry.

Hack your allocations for your Bora Bora Trip

"The best trick for saving is to eliminate the decision to save." Perry Wright of Duke University.

Put the money you plan to spend in Bora Bora on a pre-paid card in the local currency. This cuts out two problems - not knowing how much you've spent and totally avoiding expensive currency conversion fees.

You could even create separate spaces. This much for transportation, this for tours/entertainment, accommodation and food. We are reluctant to spend money that is pre-assigned to categories or uses.

Write that you want to enjoy a $3,000 trip for $500 to your Bora Bora trip. Countless research shows when you put goals in writing, you have a higher chance of following through.

Spend all the money you want to on buying experiences in Bora Bora

"Experiences are like good relatives that stay for a while and then leave. Objects are like relatives who move in and stay past their welcome." Daniel Gilbert, psychologist from Harvard University.

Economic and psychological research shows we are happier buying brief experiences on vacation rather than buying stuff to wear so give yourself freedom to spend on experiences knowing that the value you get back is many many times over.

Make saving money a game

There's one day a year where all the thrift shops where me and my family live sell everything there for a $1. My wife and I hold a contest where we take $5 and buy an entire outfit for each other. Whoever's outfit is liked more wins. We also look online to see whose outfit would have cost more to buy new. This year, my wife even snagged me an Armani coat for $1. I liked the coat when she showed it to me, but when I found out it was $500 new; I liked it and wore it a lot more.

Quadruple your money

Every-time you want to spend money, imagine it quadrupled. So the $10 you want to spend is actually $40. Now imagine that what you want to buy is four times the price. Do you still want it? If yes, go enjoy. If not, you've just saved yourself money, know you can choose to invest it in a way that quadruples or allocate it to something you really want to give you a greater return.

Understand what having unlimited amounts of money to spend in Bora Bora actually looks like

Let's look at what it would be like to have unlimited amounts of money to spend on your trip to Bora Bora.

Isolation

You take a private jet to your private Bora Bora hotel. There you are lavished with the best food, drink, and entertainment. Spending vast amounts of money on vacation equals being isolated.

If you're on your honeymoon and you want to be alone with your Amore, this is wonderful, but it can be equally wonderful to make new friends. Know this a study 'carried out by Brigham Young University, Utah found that while obesity increased risk of death by 30%, loneliness increased it by half.'

Comfort

Money can buy you late check outs of five-star hotels and priority boarding on airlines, all of which add up to comfort. But as this book has shown you, saving money in Bora Bora doesn't minimize comfort, that's just a lie travel agencies littered with glossy brochures want you to believe.

You can do late-check outs for free with the right credit cards and priority boarding can be purchased with a lot of airlines from $4. If you want to go big with first-class or business, flights offset your own travel costs by renting your own home or you can upgrade at the airport often for a fraction of what you would have paid booking a business flight online.

MORE TIPS TO FIND CHEAP FLIGHTS

"The use of travelling is to regulate imagination by reality, a nd instead of thinking how things may be, to see them as t hey are." Samuel Jackson

If you're working full-time, you can save yourself a lot of money by requesting your time off from work starting in the middle of the week. Tuesdays and Wednesdays are the cheapest days to fly. You can save thousands just by adjusting your time off.

The simplest secret to booking cheap flights is open parameters. Let's say you want to fly from Chicago to Paris. You enter the USA in from and select France under to. You may find flights from New York City to Paris for $70. Then you just need to find a cheap flight to NYC. Make sure you calculate full costs, including if you need airport accommodation and of course getting to and from airports, **but in nearly every instance open parameters will save you at least half the cost of the flight.**

If you're not sure about where you want to go, use open parameters to show you the cheapest destinations from your city. Start with skyscanner.net they include the low-cost airlines that others like Kayak leave out. Google Flights can also show you cheap destinations. To see these leave the WHERE TO section blank.

Open parameters can also show you the cheapest dates to fly. If you're flexible, you can save up to 80% of the flight cost. Always check the weather at your destination before you book. Sometimes a $400 flight will be $20, because it's monsoon season. But hey, if you like the rain, why not?

ALWAYS USE A PRIVATE BROWSER TO BOOK FLIGHTS

Skyscanner and other sites track your IP address and put prices up and down based on what they determine your strength of conviction to buy. e.g. if you've booked one-way and are looking for the return, these sites will jack the prices up by in most cases 50%. Incognito browsing pays.

Use a VPN such as Hola to book your flight from your destination

Install Hola, change your destination to the country you are flying to. The location from which a ticket is booked can affect the price significantly as algorithms consider local buying power.

Choose the right time to buy your ticket.

Choose the right time to buy your ticket, as purchasing tickets on a Sunday has been proven to be cheaper. If you can only book during the week, try to do it on a Tuesday.

Mistake fares

Email alerts from individual carriers are where you can find the best 'mistake fares". This is where a computer error has resulted in an airline offering the wrong fare. In my ex-perience, it's best to sign up to individual carriers email lists, but if you ARE lazy Secret Flying puts together a daily roster of mistake fares. Visit https://www.secretflying.com/errorfare/ to see if there're any errors that can benefit you.

Fly late for cheaper prices

Red-eye flights, the ones that leave later in the day, are typically cheaper and less crowded, so aim to book that flight if possible. You will also get through the airport much quicker at the end of the day. Just make sure there's ground transport available for when you land. You don't want to save $50 on the airfare and spend it on a taxi to your accommodation.

Use this APP for same day flights

If your plans are flexible, use 'Get The Flight Out' (http://www.gtfoflights.com/) a fare tracker Hopper that shows you same-day deeply discounted flights. This is best for long-haul flights with major carriers. You can often find a British Airways round-trip from JFK Airport to Heathrow for $300. If you booked this in advance, you'd pay at least double.

Take an empty water bottle with you

Airport prices on food and drinks are sky high. It disgusts me to see some airports charging $10 for a bottle of water. ALWAYS take an empty water bottle with you. It's relatively unknown, but most airports have drinking water fountains past the security check. Just type in your airport name to wateratairports.com to locate the fountain. Then once you've passed security (because they don't allow you to take 100ml or more of liquids) you can freely refill your bottle with water.

Round-the-World (RTW) Tickets

It is always cheaper to book your flights using a DIY approach. First, you may decide you want to stay longer in one country, and a RTW will charge you a hefty fee for changing your flight. Secondly, it all depends on where and when you travel and as we have discussed, there are many ways to ensure you pay way less than $1,500 for a year of flights. If you're travelling long-haul, the best strategy is to buy a return ticket, say New York, to Bangkok and then take cheap flights or transport around Asia and even to Australia and beyond.

Cut your costs to and from airports

Don't you hate it when getting to and from the airport is more expensive than your flight! And this is true in so many cities, especially European ones. For some reason, Google often shows the most expensive options. Use Omio to compare the cheapest transport options and save on airport transfer costs.

Car sharing instead of taxis

Check if Bora Bora has car sharing at the airport. Often they'll be tons of cars parked at the airport that are half the price of taking a taxi into the city. In most instances, you register your driving licence on an app and scan the code on the car to get going.

Checking Bags

Sometimes you need to check bags. If you do, put an Air-Tag inside. That way, you'll be about to see when you land where your bag is. This saves you the nail biting wait at baggage claim. And if worse comes to worst, and you see your bag is actually in another city, you can calmly stroll over to customer services and show them where your bag is.

Is it cheaper and more convenient to send your bags ahead?

Before you check your bags, check if it's cheaper to send them ahead of you with sendmybag.com obviously if you're staying in an Airbnb, you'll need to ask the hosts permission or you can time them to arrive the day after you. Hotels are normally very amenable.

What Credit Card Gives The Best Air Miles?

You can slash the cost of flights just for spending on a piece of plastic.

LET'S TALK ABOUT DEBT

Before we go into the best cards for each country, let's first talk about debt. The US system offers the best and biggest rewards. Why? Because they rely on the fact that many people living in the US will not pay their cards in full and the card will earn the bank significant interest payments. Other countries have a very different attitude towards money, debt, and saving than Americans. Thus in Germany and Austria the offerings aren't as favourable as the UK, Spain and Australia, where debt culture is more widely embraced. The takeaway here is this: **Only spend on one of these cards when you have set-up an automatic total monthly balance repayment. Don't let banks profit from your lizard brain!**

The best air-mile credit cards for those living in the UK

Amex Preferred Rewards Gold comes out top for those living in the UK for 2023.

Here are the benefits:

- 20,000-point bonus on £3,000 spend in first three months. These can be used towards flights with British Airways, Virgin Atlantic, Emirates and Etihad, and often

other rewards, such as hotel stays and car hire.
- 1 point per £1 spent
- 1 point = 1 airline point
- Two free visits a year to airport lounges
- No fee in year one, then £140/yr

The downside:

- Fail to repay fully and it's 59.9% rep APR interest, incl fee

You'll need to cancel before the £140/yr fee kicks in year two if you want to avoid it.

The best air-mile credit cards for those living in Canada

Aeroplan is the superior rewards program in Canada. The card has a high earn rate for Aeroplan Points, generating 1.5 points per $1 spent on eligible purchases. Look at the specifics of the eligible purchases https://www.aircanada.com/ca/en/aco/home/aeroplan/earn.html. If you're not spending on these things AMEX's Membership Rewards program offers you the best returns in Canada.

The best air-mile credit cards for those living in Germany

If you have a German bank account, you can apply for a Lufthansa credit card.

Earn 50,000 award miles if you spend $3,000 in purchases and paying the annual fee, both within the first 90 days.

Earn 2 award miles per $1 spent on ticket purchases directly from Miles & More integrated airline partners.

Earn 1 award mile per $1 spent on all other purchases.

The downsides

the €89 annual fee

Limited to fly with Lufthansa and its partners but you can capitalise on perks like the companion pass and airport lounge vouchers.

You need excellent credit to get this card.

The best air-mile credit cards for those living in Austria

"In Austria, Miles & More offers you a special credit card. You get miles for each purchase with the credit card. The Miles & More program calculates miles earned based on the distance flown and booking class. For European flights, the booking class is a flat rate. For intercontinental flights, mileage is calculated by multiplying the booking class by the distance flown." They offer a calculator so you can see how many points you could earn: https://www.miles-and-more.com/at/en/earn/airlines/mileage-calculator.html

The best air-mile credit cards for those living in Spain:

"The American Express card is the best known and oldest to earn miles, thanks to its membership Rewards program. When making payments with this card, points are added, which can then be exchanged for miles from airlines such as Iberia, Air Europa, Emirates or Alitalia." More information is available here: https://www.americanexpress.com/es-es/

The best air-mile credit cards for those living in Australia

ANZ Rewards Black comes out top for 2023.

180,000 bonus ANZ Reward Points (can get an $1,200 gift card) and $0 annual fee for the first year with the ANZ Rewards Black
Points Per Spend: 1 Velocity point on purchases of up to

$5,000 per statement period and 0.5 Velocity points there-after.
Annual Fee: $0 in the first year, then $375 after.
Ns no set minimum income required, however, there is a minimum credit limit of $15,000 on this card.

Here are some ways you can hack points onto this card: https://www.pointhacks.com.au/credit-cards/anz-rewards-black-guide/

The best air-mile credit card solution for those living in the USA with a POOR credit score

The downside to Airline Mile cards is that they require good or excellent credit scores, meaning 690 or higher.

If you have bad credit and want to use credit card air lines you will need to rebuild your credit poor. The Credit One Bank® Platinum Visa® for Rebuilding Credit is a good credit card for people with bad credit who don't want to place a deposit on a secured card. The Credit One Platinum Visa offers a $300 credit limit, rewards, and the potential for credit-limit increases, which in time will help rebuild your score.

PLEASE don't sign-up for any of these cards if you can't trust yourself to repay it in full monthly. This will only lead to stress for you.

Frequent Flyer Memberships

"Points" and "miles" are often used interchangeably, but they're usually two very different things. Maximise and diversify your rewards by utilising both.

A frequent-flyer program (FFP) is a loyalty program offered by an airline. They are designed to encourage airline customers to fly more to accumulate points (also called miles, kilometres, or segments) which can be redeemed for air travel or other rewards.

You can sign up with any FFP program for free. There are three major airline alliances in the world: Oneworld, SkyTeam and Star Alliance. I am with One World https://www.oneworld.com/members because the points can be accrued and used for most flights.

The best return on your points is to use them for international business or first class flights with lie-flat seats. You would need 3 times more miles compared to an economy flight, but if you paid cash, you'd pay 5 - 10 times more than the cost of the economy flight, so it really pays to use your points only for upgrades. The worst value for your miles is to buy an economy seat or worse, a gift from the airlines gift-shop.

Sign up for a family/household account to pool miles together. If you share a common address, you can claim the miles with most airlines. You can use AwardWallet to keep track of your miles. Remember that they only last for 2 years, so use them before they expire.

How to get 70% off a Cruise

An average cruise can set you back $4,000. If you dream of cruising the oceans, but find the pricing too high, look at repositioning cruises. You can save as much as 70% by taking a cruise which takes the boat back to its home port.

These one-way itineraries take place during low cruise seasons when ships have to reposition themselves to locations where there's warmer weather.

To find a repositioning cruise, go to vacationstogo.com/repositioning_cruises.cfm. This simple and often overlooked booking trick is great for avoiding long flights with children and can save you so much money!

It's worth noting we don't have any affiliations with any travel service or provider. The links we suggest are chosen based on our experience of finding the best deals.

Pack like a Pro

"He who would travel happily must travel light." – Antoine de St. Exupery 59.

Travel as lightly as you can. We always need less than we think. You will be very grateful that you have a light pack when changing trains, travelling through the airport, catching a bus, walking to your accommodation, or climbing stairs.

Make a list of what you will wear for 7 days and take only those clothes. You can easily wash your things while you're travelling if you stay in an Airbnb with a washing machine or visit a local laundrette. Roll your clothes for maximum space usage and fewer wrinkles. If you feel really nervous about travelling with such few things, make sure you have a dressier outfit, a little black dress for women is always valuable, a shirt for men. Then pack shorts, a long pair of pants, loose tops and a hoodie to snuggle in. Remind yourself that a lack of clothing options is an opportunity to find bargain new outfits in thrift stores. You can either sell these on eBay after you've worn them or post them home to yourself. You'll feel less stressed, as you don't have to look after or feel weighed down by excess baggage. Here are three things to remember when packing:

- Co-ordinate colours - make sure everything you bring can be worn together.

- Be happy to do laundry - fresh clothes when you're travelling feels very luxurious.

- Take liquid minis no bigger than 60ml. Liquid is heavy, and you simply don't need to carry so much at one time.

- Buy reversible clothes (coats are a great idea), dresses which can be worn multiple different ways.

Checks to Avoid Fees

Always have 6 months' validity on your passport

To enter most countries, you need 6 months from the day you land. Factor in different time zones around the world if your passport is on the edge. Airport security will stop you from boarding your flight at the airport if your passport has 5 months and 29 days left.

Google Your Flight Number before you leave for the airport

Easily find out where your plane is from anywhere. Confirm the status of your flight before you leave for the airport with flightaware.com. This can save you long unnecessary wait times.

Check-in online

The founder, Ryan O'Leary of budget airline Ryanair famously said: "We think they should pay €60 for [failing to check-in online] being so stupid.". Always check-in online, even for international flights. Cheaper international carriers like Scoot will charge you at the airport to check-in.

Checking Bags

Never, ever check a bag if you can avoid it. Sometimes you need to check bags. If you do, put an AirTag inside. That way, you'll be about to see when you land where your bag is. This saves you the nail biting wait at baggage claim. And if worse comes to worst, and you see your bag is actually in another city, you can calmly stroll over to customer services and show them where your bag is.

Is it cheaper and more convenient to send your bags ahead?

Before you check your bags, check if it's cheaper to send them ahead of you with sendmybag.com obviously if you're staying in an Airbnb, you'll need to ask the hosts permission or you can time them to arrive the day after you. Hotels are normally very amenable.

It is always cheaper to put heavier items on a ship, rather than take them on a flight with you. Find the best prices for shipping at https://www.parcelmonkey.com/delivery-services/shipping-heavy-items

Use a fragile sticker

Put a 'Fragile' sticker on anything you check to ensure that it's handled better as it goes through security. It'll also be one of the first bags released after the flight, getting you out of the airport quicker.

If you check your bag, photograph it

Take a photo of your bag before you check it. This will speed up the paperwork if it is damaged or lost.

Relaxing at the Airport

The best way to relax at the airport is in a lounge where they provide free food, drinks, comfortable chairs, luxurious amenities (many have showers) and, if you're lucky, a peaceful ambience. If you're there for a longer time, look for Airport Cubicles, sleep pods which charge by the hour.

You can use your FFP Card (Frequent Flyer Memberships) to get into select lounges for free. Check your eligibility before you pay.

If you're travelling a lot, I'd recommend investing in a Priority Pass for the airport.

It includes 850-plus airport lounges around the world. The cost is $99 for the year and $27 per lounge visit or you can pay $399 for the year all inclusive.

If you need a lounge for a one-off day, you can get a Day Pass. Buy it online for a discount, it always works out cheaper than buying at the airport. Use www.LoungePass.com.

Lounges are also great if you're travelling with kids, as they're normally free for kids and will definitely cost you less than snacks for your little ones. The rule is that kids should be seen and not heard, so consider this before taking an overly excited child who wants to run around, or you might be asked to leave even after you've paid.

Money: How to make it, spend it and save it while travelling

How to earn money WHILE travelling

"Twenty years from now you will be more disappointed by the things you didn't do than by the ones you did do. So throw off the bowlines. Sail away from the safe harbour." - H. Jackson Brown

Digital nomads receive a lot of hype. Put simply, they are " professionals who work online and therefore don't need to tie themselves to one particular office, city, or even country."

The first step in becoming a digital nomad, earning money while travelling, is knowing what you can offer. Your market is the entire world. So, what product or service would you like to offer that they would pay for? Take some time to think about this. In German, they say you should do what-ever comes easily to your hand. For example, I've always loved finding bargains, it comes easily to me. Yet I studied Law and Finance at University, which definitely did not come easy. It's not a shock that it didn't transpire into a ca-reer. And served more as a lesson in not following my ego.

There are thousands of possibilities to generate income while travelling; offering services like tutorial, coaching, writing service, PR, blogging. Most travellers I meet try their hand at blogging and earning from the advertise-ments. This is great if you have some savings, but if you need to earn straight away to travel, this should be on the back burner, as it takes time to establish. Still, if this comes easily to you, do it!

You want to make good money fast. Ask yourself, what is it you are good at and how can you deliver maximum value to other people? Here are some ideas if you're totally dum-founded:

Teaching English online - you will need a private room for this. Be aware that if you're from the USA and the country you want to work in requires a federal-level background check, it may take months, so apply early. Opportunities are on: t.vipkid.com.cn, abc360.com, italki.com, ver-balplanet.com and verbling.com. You can expect to earn $20 an hour.

Work in a hostel. Normally you'll get some cash and free accommodation.

Fruit picking. I picked Bananas in Tully, Australia for $20 an hour. The jobs are menial but can be quite meditative. Look on WWOOF.org for organic farm work. There are also amazing opportunities on worldpacker.com and work-away.com

fiverr.com - offer a small service, like making a video tem-plate and changing the content for each buyer.

Do freelance work online: marketing, finance, writing, App creation, graphic designer, UX or UI designer, SEO opti-miser / expert. Create a profile on upwork.com - you need to put in a lot of work to make this successful, but if you have a unique skill like coding or marketing, it can be very lucrative.

Make a udemy.com course. Can you offer a course in something people will pay for? e.g. stock trading, knitting or marketing.

Use Skype to deliver all manner of services: language lessons, therapy, coaching etc. Google for what you could offer. Most specialisms have a platform you can use to find clients and they will take a cut of your earnings/ require a fee.

You could work on luxury yachts in the med. It's hard work, but you can save money - DesperateSailors.com

Become an Airbnb experience host - but this requires you to know one place and stay there for a time. And you will need a work visa for that country.

Work on a cruise ship. This isn't a digital nomad job but it will help you travel and save at the same time.

Rent your place out on Airbnb while you travel and get a cleaner to manage it. The easiest solution if you own or have a long-term rent contract.

Passive Income Ideas that earn $1000+ a month

- Start a YouTube Channel.

- Start a Membership Website.

- Write a Book.

- Create a Lead Gen Website for Service Businesses.

- Join the Amazon Affiliate Program.

- Market a Niche Affiliate Opportunity.

- Create an Online Course.

- Invest in Real Estate

How to spend money

Bank ATM fees vary from $2.50 per transaction to as high as $5 or more, depending on the ATM and the country. You can completely skip those fees by paying with card and using a card which can hold multiple currencies.

Budget travel hacking begins with a strategy to spend without fees. Your individual strategy depends on the country you legally reside in as to what cards are available. Happily there are some fin-tech solutions which can save you thousands on those pesky ATM withdrawal fees and are widely available globally. Here are a selection of cards you can pre-charge with currency for Bora Bora:

N26

N26 is a 12-year-old digital bank. I have been using them for over 6 years. The key advantage is fee-free card transactions abroad. They have a very elegant app, where you can check your timeline for all transactions listed in real time or manage your in-app security anywhere. The card you receive is a Mastercard so you can use it everywhere. If you lose the card, you don't have to call anyone, just open the app and swipe 'lock card'. It puts your purchases into a graph automatically so you can see what you spend on. You can open an account from abroad entirely online, all you need is your passport and a camera n26.com

Revolut

Revolut is a multi-currency account that allows you to hold and exchange 29 currencies and spend fee-free abroad. It's a UK based neobank, but accepts customers from all over the world.

Wise debit card

If you're going to be in one place for a long time, the Wise debit card is like having your travel money on a card – it lets you spend money at the real exchange rate.

Monzo

Monzo is good if your UK based. They offer a fee-free UK account. Fee-free international money transfers and fee-free spending abroad.

The downside

The cards above are debit cards, meaning you need to have money in those accounts to spend it. This comes with one big downside: safety. Credit card issuers' have "zero liability" meaning you're not liable for unauthorised charges. All the cards listed above do provide cover for unauthorised charges but times vary greatly in how quickly you'd get your money back if it were stolen.

The best option is to check in your country to see which credit cards are the best for travelling and set up monthly payments to repay the whole amount so you don't pay unnecessary interest. In the USA, Schwab regularly ranks at the top for travel credit cards. Credit cards are always the safer option when abroad simply because you get your money back faster if its stolen and if you're renting cars, most will give you free insurance when you book the car rental using the card, saving you money.

Always withdraw money; never exchange.

Money exchanges, whether they be on the streets or in the airports will NEVER give you a good exchange rate. Do not bring bundles of cash. Instead, withdraw local currency from the ATM as needed and try to use only free ATMs. Many in airports charge you a fee to withdraw cash. Look for bigger ATMs attached to banks to avoid this.

Recap

- Take cash from local, non-charging ATMs for the best rates.

- Never change at airport exchange desks unless you absolutely have to, then just change just enough to be able get to a bank ATM.

- Bring a spare credit card for emergencies.

- Split cash in various places on your person (pockets, shoes) and in your luggage. It's never sensible to keep your cash or cards all in one place.

- In higher risk areas, use a money belt under your clothes or put $50 in your shoe or bra.

Revolut

Revolut is a multi-currency account that allows you to hold and exchange 29 currencies and spend fee-free abroad. It's a UK based neobank, but accepts customers from all over the world.

Wise debit card

If you're going to be in one place for a long time the Wise debit card is like having your travel money on a card – it lets you spend money at the real exchange rate.

Monzo

Monzo is good if your UK based. They offer a fee-free UK account. Fee-free international money transfers and fee-free spending abroad.

The downside

The cards above are debit cards, meaning you need to have money in those accounts to spend it. This comes with one big downside: safety. Credit card issuers' have "zero liability" meaning you're not liable for unauthorised charges. All of the cards listed above do provide cover for unauthorised charges but times vary greatly in how quickly you'd get your money back if it were stolen.

The best option is to check in your country to see which credit cards are the best for travelling and set up monthly payments to repay the whole amount so you don't pay un-necessary interest. In the USA, Schwab[2] regularly ranks at the top for travel credit cards. Credit cards are always the safer option when abroad simply because you get your

---

[2] Charles Schwab High Yield Checking accounts refund every single ATM fee worldwide, require no minimum balance and have no monthly fee.

money back faster if its stolen and if you're renting cars, most will give you free insurance when you book the car rental using the card, saving you money.

Always withdraw money; never exchange.

Money exchanges whether they be on the streets or in the airports will NEVER give you a good exchange rate. Do not bring bundles of cash. Instead withdraw local currency from the ATM as needed and try to use only free ATM's. Many in airports charge you a fee to withdraw cash. Look for bigger ATM's attached to banks to avoid this.

Recap

- Take cash from local, non-charging ATMs for the best rates.
- Never change at airport exchange desks unless you absolutely have to, then just change just enough to be able get to a bank ATM.
- Bring a spare credit card for emergencies.
- Split cash in various places on your person (pockets, shoes) and in your luggage. Its never sensible to keep your cash or cards all in one place.
- In higher risk areas, use a money belt under your clothes or put $50 in your shoe or bra.

How to save money while travelling

Saving money while travelling sounds like an oxymoron, but it can be done with little to no effort. Einstein is credited as saying, "Compound interest is the eighth wonder of the world." If you saved and invested $100 today, in 20 years, it would be $2,000 thanks to the power of compound interest. It makes sense then to save your money, invest and make even more money.

The Acorns app is a simple system for this. It rounds up your credit card purchases and puts the rest into a savings account. So if you pay for a coffee and its $3.01, you'll save 0.99 cents. You won't even notice you're saving by using this app: www.acorns.com

Here are some more generic ways you can always save money while travelling:

Device Safety

Having your phone, iPad or laptop stolen is one BIG and annoying way you can lose money travelling. The simple solution is to use apps to track your devices. Some OSes have this feature built-in. Prey will try your smartphones or laptops (preyproject.com).

Book New Airbnb's

When you take a risk on a new Airbnb listing, you save money. Just make sure the hosts profile is at least 3 years old and has reviews.

If you end up in an overcrowded city

The website https://campspace.com/ is like Airbnb for camping in people's garden and is a great way to save money if you end up in a city during a big event.

Look out for free classes

Lots of hostels offer free classes for guests. If you're planning to stay in a hostel, check out what classes your hostel offers. I have learnt languages, cooking techniques, dance styles, drawing and all manner of things for free by taking advantage of free classes at hostels.

Get student discounts

If you're studying buy an ISIC card - International Student Identity Card. It is internationally recognised, valid in 133 countries and offers more than 150,000 discounts!

Get Senior Citizen discounts

Most state run attractions, ie, museums, galleries will offer a discount for people over 65 with ID.

Instal maps.me

Maps me is extremely good for travelling without data. It's like offline google maps without the huge download size.

Always buy travel insurance

Don't travel without travel insurance. It is a small cost to pay compared with what could be a huge medical bill.

Travel Apps That'll Make Budget Travel Easier

Travel apps are useful for booking and managing travel logistics. They have one fatal downside: they can track you in the app and keep prices up. If you face this, access the site from an incognito browser tab.

Here are the best apps and what they can do for you:

- Best For flight Fare-Watching: Hopper.

- Best for booking flights: Skyscanner and Google Flights

- Best for timing airport arrivals: FlightAware - check on delays, cancellations and gate changes.

- Best for overcoming a fear of flying: SkyGuru - turbulence forecasts for the route you're flying.

- Best for sharing your location: TripWhistle - text or send your GPS coordinates or location easily.

- Best for splitting expenses among co-travellers: Splittr, Trip Splitter, Venmo or Splitwise.

How NOT to be ripped off

"One of the great things about travel is that you find out ho
w many good, kind people there are."
— Edith Wharton

The quote above may seem ill placed in a chapter entitled
how not to be ripped off, but I included it to remind you
that the vast majority of people do not want to rip you off.
In fact, scammers are normally limited to three situations:

1. Around heavily visited attractions - these places are
    targeted purposively due to sheer footfall. Many
    criminals believe ripping people off is simply a num-
    bers game.

2. In cities or countries with low-salaries or communist
    ideologies. If they can't make money in the country,
    they seek to scam foreigners. If you have travelled to
    India, Morocco or Cuba you will have observed this
    phenomenon.

3. When you are stuck and the person helping you
    know you have limited options.

Scammers know that most people will avoid confrontation.
Don't feel bad about utterly ignoring someone and saying
no. Here are six strategies to avoid being ripped off:

1. **Never ever agree to pay as much as you want.
    Always decide on a price before.**

Whoever you're dealing with is trained to tell you, they are
uninterested in money. This is a trap. If you let people do

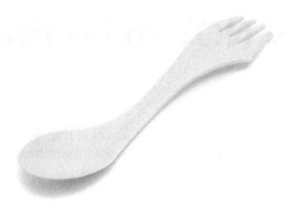

this they will ask for MUCH MORE money at the end, and because you have used there service, you will feel obliged to pay. This is a conman's trick and nothing more.

2. Pack light

You can move faster and easier. If you take heavy luggage, you will end up taking taxis which are comparatively very costly over time.

3. NEVER use the airport taxi service. Plan to use public transport before you reach the airport.

4. Don't buy a sim card from the airport. Buy from the local supermarkets it will cost 50% less.

5. Eat at local restaurants serving regional food

Food defines culture. Exploring all delights available to the palate doesn't need to cost enormous sums.

6. Ask the locals what something should cost, and try not to pay over that.

7. If you find yourself with limited options. e.g. your taxi dumps you on the side of the road because you refuse to pay more (common in India and parts of South America) don't act desperate and negotiate as if you have other options or you will be extorted.

8. Don't blindly rely on social media[3]

Let's say you post in a Facebook group that you want tips for travelling to The Maldives. A lot of the comments you will receive come from guides, hosts and restaurants doing their own promotion. It's estimated that 50% or more of Facebook's current monthly active users are fake. And what's worse, a recent study found Social media platforms leave 95% of reported fake accounts up. These accounts are the digital versions of the men who hang around the Grand Palace in Bangkok telling tourists its closed, to divert you to shops where they will receive a commission for bringing you.

It can also be the case that genuine comments come from people who have totally different interests, beliefs and yes, budgets to yours. Make your experience your own and don't believe every comment you read.

Bottom line: use caution when accepting recommendations on social media and always fact-check with your own research.

Small tweaks on the road add up to big differences in your bank balance

Take advantage of other hotel amenities

If you fancy a swim but you're nowhere near the ocean, try the nearest hotel with a pool. As long as you buy a drink, the hotel staff will probably grant you access.

Fill up your mini bar for free.

---

[3] https://arstechnica.com/tech-policy/2019/12/social-media-platforms-leave-95-of-reported-fake-accounts-up-study-finds/

Fill up your mini bar for free by storing things from the breakfast bar or grocery shop in your mini bar to give you a greater selection of drinks and food without the hefty price tag.

Save yourself some ironing

Use the steam from the shower to get rid of wrinkles in clothing. If something is creased, leave it trapped with the steam in the bathroom overnight for even better results.

See somewhere else for free

Opt for long stopovers, allowing you to experience another city without spending much money.

Wear your heaviest clothes

On the plane to save weight in your pack, allowing you to bring more with you. Big coats can then be used as pillows to make your flight more comfortable.

Don't get lost while you're away.

Find where you want to go using Google Maps, then type 'OK Maps' into the search bar to store this information for offline viewing.

Use car renting services

Share Now or Car2Go allow you to hire a car for 2 hours for $25 in a lot of European countries.

Share Rides

Use sites like blablacar.com to find others who are driving in your direction. It can be 80% cheaper than normal transport. Just check the drivers reviews.

Use free gym passes

Get a free gym day pass by googling the name of a local gym and free day pass.

When asked by people providing you a service where you are from..

If there's no price list for the service you are asking for, when asked where you are from, Say you are from a lesser-known poorer country. I normally say Macedonia, and if they don't know where it is, add it's a poor country. If you say UK, USA, the majority of Europe bar the well-known poorer countries taxi drivers, tour operators etc will match the price to what they think you pay at home.

Set-up a New Uber/ other car hailing app account for discounts

By googling you can find offers with $50 free for new users in most cities for Uber/ Lyft/ Bolt and alike. Just set up a new gmail.com email account to take advantage.

Where and How to Make Friends

"People don't take trips, trips take people." – John Steinbeck

Become popular at the airport

Want to become popular at the airport? Pack a power bar with multiple outlets and just see how many friends you can make. It's amazing how many people forget their chargers, or who packed them in the luggage that they checked in.

Stay in Hostels

First of all, Hostels don't have to be shared dorms, and they cater to a much wider demographic than is assumed. Hostels are a better environment for meeting people than hotels, and more importantly, they tended to open up excursion opportunities that further opened up that opportunity.

Or take up a hobby

If hostels are a definite no-no for you; find an interest. Take up a hobby where you will meet people. I've dived for years and the nature of diving is you're always paired up with a dive buddy. I met a lot of interesting people that way.

Small tweaks on the road add up to big differences in your bank balance

Take advantage of other hotel's amenities

If you fancy a swim but you're nowhere near the ocean, try the nearest hotel with a pool. As long as you buy a drink, the hotel staff will likely grant you access.

Fill up your mini bar for free.

Fill up your mini bar for free by storing things from the breakfast bar or grocery shop in your mini bar to give you a greater selection of drinks and food without the hefty price tag.

Save yourself some ironing

Use the steam from the shower to get rid of wrinkles in clothing. If something is creased, leave it trapped with the steam in the bathroom overnight for even better results.

See somewhere else for free

Opt for long stopovers, allowing you to experience another city without spending much money.

Wear your heaviest clothes

on the plane to save weight in your pack, allowing you to bring more with you. Big coats can then be used as pillows to make your flight more comfortable.

Don't get lost while you're away.

Find where you want to go using Google Maps, then type 'OK Maps' into the search bar to store this information for offline viewing.

Use car renting services

Share Now or Car2Go allow you to hire a car for 2 hours for $25 in a lot of Europe.

Share Rides

Use sites like blablacar.com to find others who are driving in your direction. It can be 80% cheaper than normal transport. Just check the drivers reviews.

Use free gym passes

Get a free gym day pass by googling the name of a local gym and free day pass.

When asked by people providing you a service where you are from..

If there's no price list for the service you are asking for, when asked where you are from, Say you are from a lesser-known poorer country. I normally say Macedonia, and if they don't know where it is, add it's a poor country. If you say UK, USA, the majority of Europe bar the well-known poorer countries taxi drivers, tour operators etc will match the price to what they think you pay at home.

Set-up a New Uber/ other car hailing app account for discounts

By googling you can find offers with $50 free for new users in most cities for Uber/ Lyft/ Bolt and alike. Just set up a new gmail.com email account to take advantage.

Where and How to Make Friends

"People don't take trips, trips take people." – John Steinbeck

Become popular at the airport

Want to become popular at the airport? Pack a power bar with multiple outlets and just see how many friends you can make. It's amazing how many people forget their chargers, or who packed them in the luggage that they checked in.

Stay in Hostels

First of all, Hostels don't have to be shared dorms, and they cater to a much wider demographic than is assumed. Hostels are a better environment for meeting people than hotels, and more importantly they tended to open up excursion opportunities that further opened up that opportunity.

Or take up a hobby

If hostels are a definite no-no for you; find an interest. Take up a hobby where you will meet people. I've dived for years and the nature of diving is you're always paired up with a dive buddy. I met a lot of interesting people that way.

When unpleasantries come your way...

We all have our good and bad days travelling, and on a bad day you can feel like just taking a flight home. Here are some ways to overcome common travel problems:

Anxiety when flying

It has been over 40 years since a plane has been brought down by turbulence. Repeat that number to yourself: 40 years! Planes are built to withstand lighting strikes, extreme storms and ultimately can adjust course to get out of their way. Landing and take-off are when the most accidents happen, but you have statistically three times the chance of winning a huge jackpot lottery, then you do of dying in a plane crash.

If you feel afraid on the flight, focus on your breathing saying the word 'smooth' over and over until the flight is smooth. Always check the airline safety record on airlinerating.com I was surprised to learn Ryanair and Easyjet as much less safe than Wizz Air according to those ratings because they sell similarly priced flights. If there is extreme turbulence, I feel much better knowing I'm in a 7 star safety plane.

Wanting to sleep instead of seeing new places

This is a common problem. Just relax, there's little point doing fun things when you feel tired. Factor in jet-lag to your travel plans. When you're rested and alert you'll enjoy your new temporary home much more. Many people hate the first week of a long-trip because of jet-lag and often blame this on their first destination, but its rarely true. Ask travellers who 'hate' a particular place and you will see that very often they either had jet-lag or an unpleasant journey there.

Going over budget

Come back from a trip to a monster credit card bill? Hopefully, this guide has prevented you from returning to an unwanted bill. Of course, there are costs that can creep up and this is a reminder about how to prevent them making their way on to your credit card bill:

- To and from the airport. Solution: leave adequate time and take the cheapest method - book before.

- Baggage. Solution: take hand luggage and post things you might need to yourself.

- Eating out. Solution: go to cheap eats places and suggest those to friends.

- Parking. Solution: use apps to find free parking

- Tipping. Solution Leave a modest tip and tell the server you will write them a nice review.

- Souvenirs. Solution: fridge magnets only.

- Giving to the poor. (This one still gets me, but if you're giving away $10 a day - it adds up) Solution: volunteer your time instead and recognise that in tourist destinations many beggars are run by organised crime gangs.

Price v Comfort

I love traveling. I don't love struggling. I like decent accommodation, being able to eat properly and see places and enjoy. I am never in the mood for low-cost airlines or crappy transfers, so here's what I do to save money.

- Avoid organised tours unless you are going to a place where safety is a real issue. They are expensive and constrain your wanderlust to typical things. I only recommend them in Algeria, Iran and Papua New Guinea - where language and gender views pose serious problems all cured by a reputable tour organiser.

- Eat what the locals do.

- Cook in your Airbnb/ hostel where restaurants are expensive.

- Shop at local markets.

- Spend time choosing your flight, and check the operator on arilineratings.com

- Mix up hostels and Airbnbs. Hostels for meeting people, Airbnb for relaxing and feeling 'at home'.

Not knowing where free toilets are

Use Toilet Finder - https://play.google.com/store/apps/details?id=com.bto.toilet&hl=en

Your Airbnb is awful

Airbnb customer service is notoriously bad. Help yourself out. Try to sort things out with the host, but if you can't, take photos of everything e.g bed, bathroom, mess, doors, contact them within 24 hours. Tell them you had to leave and pay for new accommodation. Ask politely for a full refund including booking fees. With photographic evidence and your new accommodation receipt, they can't refuse.

The airline loses your bag

Go to the Luggage desk before leaving the airport and report the bag missing. Hopefully you've headed the advice to put an AirTag in your checked bag and you can show them where to find your bag. Most airlines will give you an overnight bag, ask where you're staying and return the bag to you within three days. It's extremely rare for Airlines to lose your bag due to technological innovation, but if that happens you should submit an insurance claim after the three days is up, including receipts for everything you had to buy in the interim.

Your travel companion lets you down

Whether it's a breakup or a friend cancelling, it sucks and can ramp up costs. The easiest solution to finding a new travel companion is to go to a well-reviewed hostel and find someone you want to travel with. You should spend at least three days getting to know this person before you suggest travelling together. Finding someone in person is always better than finding someone online, because you can get a better idea of whether you will have a smooth journey together. Travel can make or break friendships.

Culture shock

I had one of the strongest culture shocks while spending 6 months in Japan. It was overwhelming how much I had to prepare when I went outside of the door (googling words and sentences what to use, where to go, which station and train line to use, what is this food called in Japanese and how does its look etc.). I was so tired constantly but in the end I just let go and went with my extremely bad Japanese. If you feel culture shocked its because your brain is referencing your surroundings to what you know. Stop comparing, have Google translate downloaded and relax.

Your Car rental insurance is crazy expensive

I always use carrentals.com and book with a credit card.
Most credit cards will give you free insurance for the car, so
you don't need to pay the extra. Some unsavoury companies will bump the price up when you arrive. Ask to speak
to a manager. If this doesn't resolve, it google "consumer
ombudsman for NAME OF COUNTRY." and seek an immediate full refund on the balance difference you paid. It is il-
legal in most countries to alter the price of a rental car
when the person arrives to pickup a pre-arranged car.

A note on Car Rental Insurance

Always always always rent a car with a credit card that has
rental vehicle coverage built into the card and is automatically applied when you rent a car. Then there's no need to
buy additional rental insurance (check with your card on
the coverage they protect some exclude collision coverage). Do yourself a favour when you step up to the desk to
rent the car tell the agent you're already covered and won't
be buying anything today. They work on commission and
you'll save time and your patience avoiding the upselling.

You're sick

First off ALWAYS, purchase travel insurance. Including
emergency transport up to $500k even to back home,
which is usually less than $10 additional. I use https://
www.comparethemarket.com/travel-insurance/ to find the
best days. If I am sick I normally check into a hotel with
room service and ride it out.

Make a Medication Travel Kit

Take travel sized medications with you:

- Antidiarrheal medication (for example, bismuth sub-salicylate, loperamide)

- Medicine for pain or fever (such as acetaminophen, aspirin, or ibuprofen)

- Throat Lozenges

Save yourself from most travel related hassles

- Do not make jokes with immigration and customs staff. A misunderstanding can lead to HUGE fines.

- Book the most direct flight you can find nonstop if possible.

- Carry a US$50 bill for emergency cash. I have entered a country and all ATM and credit card systems were down. US$ can be exchanged nearly anywhere in the world and is useful in extreme situations, but where possible don't exchange, as you will lose money.

- Check, and recheck, required visas and such BE-FORE the day of your trip. Some countries, for instance, require a ticket out of the country in order to enter. Others, like the US and Australia, require electronic authorisation in advance.

- Airport security is asinine and inconsistent around the world. Keep this in mind when connecting flights. Always leave at least 2 hours for international connections or international to domestic. In Stansted for example, they force you to buy one of their plastic bags, and remove your liquids from your own plastic bag.... just to make money from you. And this adds to the time it will take to get through security, so lines are long.

- Wiki travel is perfect to use for a lay of the land.

- Expensive luggage rarely lasts longer than cheap luggage, in my experience. Fancy leather bags are toast with air travel.

Food

- When it comes to food, eat in local restaurants, not tourist-geared joints. Any place with the menu in three or more languages is going to be overpriced.

- Take a spork - a knife, spoon and fork all in one.

Water Bottle

Take a water bottle with a filter. We love these ones from Water to Go.

Empty it before airport security and separate the bottle and filter as some airport people will try and claim it has liquids...

Bug Sprays

If you're heading somewhere tropical spray your clothes with Permethrin before you travel. It lasts 40 washes and saves space in your bag. A 'Bite Away' zapper can be used after the bite to totally erase it. It cuts down on the itching and erases the bite from your skin.

Order free mini's

Don't buy those expensive travel sized toiletries, order travel sized freebies online. This gives you the opportunity to try brands you've never used before, and who knows, you might even find your new favourite soap.

Take a waterproof bag

If you're travelling alone you can swim without worrying about your phone, wallet and passport laying on the beach.

You can also use it as a source of entertainment on those ultra budget flights.

Make a private entertainment centre anywhere

Always take an eye-mask, earplugs, a scarf and a kindle reader - so you can sleep and entertain yourself anywhere!

The best Travel Gadgets

The door alarm

If you're nervous and staying in private rooms or airbnbs take a door alarm. For those times when you just don't feel safe, it can help you fall asleep. You can get tiny ones for less than $10 from Amazon: https://www.amazon.com/Travel-door-alarm/s?k=Travel+door+alarm

Smart Blanket

Amazon sells a 6 in 1 heating blanket that is very useful for cold plane or bus trips. Its great if you have poor circulation as it becomes a detachable Foot Warmer: Amazon http://amzn.to/2hTYIOP I paid $49.00.

The coat that becomes a tent

https://www.adiff.com/products/tent-jacket. This is great if you're going to be doing a lot of camping.

Clever Tank Top with Secret Pockets

Keep your valuables safe in this top. Perfect for all climates.
                                    on Amazon for $39.90

Optical Camera Lens for Smartphones and Tablets

Leave your bulky camera at home. Turn your device into a high-performance camera. Buy on Amazon for $9.95

Travel-sized Wireless Router with USB Media Storage

Convert any wired network to a wireless network. Buy on Amazon for $17.99

Buy a Scrubba Bag to wash your clothes on the go

Or a cheaper imitable. You can wash your clothes on the go.

Hacks for Families

Rent an Airbnb apartment so you can cook

Apartments are much better for families, as you have all the amenities you'd have at home. They are normally cheaper per person too. We are the first travel guide publisher to include Airbnb's in our recommendations if you think any of these need updating you can email me at philgtang@gmail.com

Shop at local markets

Eat seasonal products and local products. Get closer to the local market and observe the prices and the offer. What you can find more easily, will be the cheapest.

Take Free Tours

Download free podcast tours of the destination you are visiting. The podcast will tell you where to start, where to go, and what to look for. Often you can find multiple podcast tours of the same place. Listen to all of them if you like, each one will tell you a little something new.

Pack Extra Ear Phones

If you go on a museum tour, they often have audio guides. Instead of having to rent one for each person, take some extra earphones. Most audio tour devices have a place to plug in a second set.

Buy Souvenirs Ahead of Time

If you are buying souvenirs somewhere touristy, you are paying a premium price. By ordering the same exact products online, you can save a lot of money.

Use Cheap Transportation

Do as the locals do, including weekly passes.

Carry Reusable Water Bottles

Spending money on water and other beverages can quickly add up. Instead of paying for drinks, take some refillable water bottles.

Combine Attractions

Many major cities offer ticket bundles where one price gets you into 5 or 6 popular attractions. You will need to plan ahead of time to decide what things you plan to do on vacation and see if they are selling these activities together.

Pack Snacks

Granola bars, apples, baby carrots, bananas, cheese crackers, juice boxes, pretzels, fruit snacks, apple sauce, grapes, and veggie chips.

Stick to Carry-On Bags

Do not pay to check a large bag. Even a small child can pull a carry-on.

Visit free art galleries and museums

Just google the name + free days.

Eat Street Food

There's a lot of unnecessary fear around this. You can watch the food prepared. Go for the stands that have a steady queue.

Travel Gadgets for Families

Dropcam

Are what-if scenarios playing out in your head? Then you need Dropcam.

'Dropcam HD Internet Wi-Fi Video Monitoring Cameras help you watch what you love from anywhere. In less than a minute, you'll have it setup and securely streaming video to you over your home Wi-Fi. Watch what you love while away with Dropcam HD.'

Approximate Price: $139

Kelty-Child-Carrier

Voted as one of the best hiking essentials if you're traveling with kids and can carry a child up to 18kg.

Jetkids Bedbox

No more giving up your own personal space on the plane with this suitcase that becomes a bed.

Safety

"If you think adventure is dangerous, try routine. It's lethal." – Paulo Coelho

Backpacker murdered is a media headline that leads people to think traveling is more dangerous than it is. The media sensationalise the rare murders and deaths of backpackers and travellers. The actual chances of you dying abroad are extremely extremely low.

Let's take the USA as an example. In 2018, 724 Americans **died** from unnatural causes, 167 died from car accidents, while the majority of the other deaths resulted from drownings, suicides, and non-vehicular accidents. Contrast this with the 15,000 murders in the US in 2018, and travelling abroad looks much safer than staying at home.

There are many things you can to keep yourself safe. Here are our tips.

1. Always check fco.co.uk before travelling. NEVER RELY on websites or books. Things are changing constantly and the FCO's (UK's foreign office) advice is always UP TO DATE (hourly) and **extremely conservative**.

2. Check your mindset. I've travelled alone to over 180 countries and the main thing I learnt is if you walk around scared, or anticipating you're going to be pickpocketed, your constant fear will attract bad energy. Murders or attacks on travellers are the mainstay of media, not reality, especially in countries familiar with travellers. The only place I had cause to genuinely fear for my life was Papua New Guinea -

where nothing actually happened to me only my own panic over culture shock.

There are many things you can do to stop yourself being victim to the two main problems when travelling: theft or being scammed.

I will address theft first. Here are my top tips:

- Stay alert while you're out and always have an exit strategy.

- Keep your money in a few different places on your person and your passport somewhere it can't be grabbed.

- Take a photo of your passport on your phone in case. If you do lose it, google for your embassy, you can usually get a temporary pretty fast.

- Google safety tips for travelling in your country to help yourself out and memorise the emergency number.

- At hostels, keep your large bag in the room far under the bed/out of the way with a lock on the zipper.

- On buses/trains, I would even lock my bag to the luggage rack.

- Get a personal keychain alarm. The sound will scare anyone away.

- Don't wear any jewellery. A man attempted to rob a friend of her engagement ring in Bogota, Colombia, and in hindsight I wished I'd told her to leave it at home/wear it on a hidden necklace, as the chaos it created was avoidable.

- Don't turn your back to traffic while you use your phone.

- When travelling in the tuktuk sit in the middle and keep your bag secure. Wear sunglasses as dust can easily get in your eyes.

- Don't let anyone give you flowers, bracelets, or any type of trinket, even if they insist it's for free and compliment you like crazy.

- Don't let strangers know that you are alone - unless they are travel friends ;-)

- Lastly, and most importantly -Trust your gut! If it doesn't feel right, it isn't.

How I got hooked on budget travelling

'We're on holiday' is what my dad used to say to justify getting us in so much debt we lost our home and all our things when I was 11. We moved from the suburban bliss of Hemel Hempstead to a run down council estate in inner-city London, near my dad's new job as a refuge collector, a fancy word for dustbin man. I lost all my school friends while watching my dad go through a nervous breakdown.

My dad loved walking up a hotel lobby desk without a care in the world. So much so, that he booked overpriced holidays on credit cards. A lot of holidays. As it turned out, we couldn't afford any of them. In the end, my dad had no choice but to declare bankruptcy. When my mum realised, he'd racked up so much debt our family unit dissolved. A neat and perhaps as painless a summary of events that lead me to my life's passion: budget travel that doesn't compromise on fun, safety or comfort.

I started travelling full-time at the age of 18. I wrote the first Super Cheap Insider guide for friends visiting Norway - which I did for a month on less than $250. When sales reached 10,000 I decided to form the Super Cheap Insider Guides company. As I know from first-hand experience debt can be a noose around our necks, and saying 'oh come on, we're on vacation' isn't a get out of jail free card. In fact, its the reverse of what travel is supposed to bring you - freedom.

Before I embarked upon writing Super Cheap Insider guides, many, many people told me that my dream was impossible. Travelling on a budget could never be comfortable. I hope this guide has proved to you what I have known for a long-time: budget travel can feel luxurious when you know and use the insider hacks.

And apologies if I depressed you with my tale of woe. My dad is now happily remarried and works as a chef in London at a fancy hotel - the kind he used to take us to!

A final word...

There's a simple system you can use to think about budget travel. In life, we can choose two of the following: cheap, fast, or quality. So if you want it Cheap and fast you will get a lower quality service. Fast-food is the perfect example. The system holds true for purchasing anything while travelling. I always choose cheap and quality, except at times where I am really limited on time. Normally, you can make small tweaks to make this work for you. Ultimately, you must make choices about what's most important to you and heed your heart's desires.

'Your heart is the most powerful muscle in your body. Do what it says.' Jen Sincero

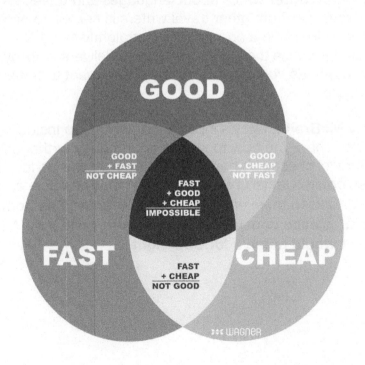

Our Writers

Phil Tang was born in London to Irish immigrant, Phil graduated from The London School of Economics with a degree in Law. Now he travels full-time in search of travel bargains with his wife, dog and a baby and a toddler.

Ali Blythe has been writing about amazing places for 17 years. He loves travel and especially tiny budgets equalling big adventures nearly as much as his family. He recently trekked the Satopanth Glacier trekking through those ways from where no one else would trek. Ali is an adventurer by nature and bargainist by religion.

Michele Whitter writes about languages and travel. What separates her from other travel writers is her will to explain complex topics in a no-nonsense, straightforward way. She doesn't promise the world. But always delivers step-by-step methods you can immediately implement to travel on a budget.

Lizzy McBraith, Lizzy's input on Super Cheap Insider Guides show you how to stretch your money further so you can travel cheaper, smarter, and with more wanderlust. She loves going over land on horses and helps us refine each guide to keep them effective. **If you've found this book useful, please consider leaving a short review on Amazon. it would mean a lot.Copyright**

If you've found this book useful, please select five stars on Amazon, it would mean genuinely make my day to see I've helped you.

Copyright

Published in Great Britain in 2023 by Super Cheap Insider Guides LTD.

Copyright © 2023 Super Cheap Insider Guides LTD.

The right of Phil G A Tang to be identified as the Author of the Work has been asserted in accordance with the Copyright, Designs and Patents Act 1988.

Made in the USA
Las Vegas, NV
10 December 2023

82444334R00100